MACBUSH

By the same author

BURNT TOAST

(A. A. Knopf, 1971)

A PEASANT OF EL SALVADOR

(With Stephen Stearns)

(Whetstone Books, 1983)

MACBUSH

A Comedy in Five Acts

by

Peter Gould

WHETSTONE BOOKS

Brattleboro, Vermont

ISBN 0-915731-02-9

Book Design by Martha Raines
Cover cartoon by Paul Szep

Manufactured in the United States of America

WHETSTONE BOOKS
22 West St.
Brattleboro, Vt. 05301

Acknowledgements: To Mollie Burke, with love, To The Brooks Memorial Library, Brattleboro, Vermont: for office space and research help. To Dan Wasserman, for the battle cry on page 99. To Bonnie and Stephen Stearns, for encouragement. To the Bard of Avon.

DISCLAIMER

"MACBUSH, A Comedy in Five Acts" is dramatic fiction. Any resemblance between its characters and any well-known actual men and women is a coincidence. But what a coincidence!

This is the original version of "MACBUSH", as written by Peter Gould from November, 1986 through December, 1987. In the case of "MACBETH," nearly twenty years elapsed from the time that Shakespeare wrote the play, till its first publication. Meanwhile, a generation of actors and directors, in rehearsals and performances, doubtless improved the script, brought it to the perfection in which we read it today.

Alas, I can't wait twenty years. Not twenty days, not twenty minutes. Peddlers line up to hawk this edition on the streets, even while actors, scripts in hand, walk through their parts for the first time. Eventually, they will improve the play.

> *Good friends, for Jesus' sake forebear*
> *To change too much what's written here.*
> *Blessed be ye if fault you find,*
> *And cursed be ye who change good lines.*

For Barbara Garson,
who lit the way

DRAMATIS PERSONAE

RONALD, A King
HIS CHIEF OF STAFF
HIS ADVISOR
NORTH, An Officer
A SPOKESMAN

MACBUSH, The King's Right-Hand Man
LADY MACBUSH, His Wife
AIDE, To Macbush
SERVANT, To Lady Macbush
WOMAN, Servant to Lady Macbush

MACDOLE, A Nobleman
KEMPF, Another Nobleman
A SENATOR

A SCIENTIST/SPY
DOCTOR, A Psychiatrist

A HOMELESS MAN
A HOMELESS WOMAN

FIRST TELEVANGELIST
SECOND TELEVANGELIST
THIRD TELEVANGELIST
WOMAN, Their Receptionist
GOD, An Invisible Divinity

THREE LATIN-AMERICAN PEASANTS
A SOLDIER, Attendant on Them
PRIEST, A Liberation Theologian

FISHERMAN, A Maine Lobsterman
JUAN GARCIA, A Spy & Covert-Op

LADY MACDOLE

VARIOUS Courtiers, Attendants,
Advisors, Guests

PROLOGUE

(Spoken by a Homeless Woman)

Fine ladies, well-dressed gentlemen, excuse
The sad state of our clothes, our hair, our smell—
We people bedded in the street
Are not unconscious, though we seem to sleep.
You cannot lie, ear pressed to th' ground, without
You hear the tramp of feet, the swift rumors
That course the Metro tunnels, or beat the air.
Therefore we know the gist of what's to come,
And know, also, the brave poet who penned
These lines forgot the most important part:
The apology. The minstrels always used
To beg forgiveness before they spoke the truth
In songs and one-liners, lest the axe fall
Or th' leg irons clamp shut.
Our poet, though he said it not, is sorry—
Not so much for the words he wrote, and which
The actors stand about to speak, but for
His times, the men, the situation, which
Demand that he revive old ghosts and dress 'em
In modern clothes. When high and mighty men
Grapple for power, it's the same old story:
New names, new faces, in a plot grown hoary.
All this the poet knows, yet knows not well
Enough to resist the urge to tell the tale.

ACT I

☆☆☆☆

SCENE 1

(A board room in a TV studio. Popular easy-listening Christian music playing. Enter THREE TELEVISION MINISTERS. They are carrying attaché cases. All three are white, middle-aged males impeccably dressed in polyester suits.)

FIRST TELEVANGELIST: When shall we three meet again?

SECOND TELEVANGELIST: Honduras, Libya, or Iran?

THIRD TELEVANGELIST: Wherever covert action's done: there the battle's lost or won.

FIRST TELEVANGELIST: Amen.

SECOND TELEVANGELIST: Meanwhile I'll go hand out these funds.

THIRD TELEVANGELIST: And I'll come, too. We'll take my plane. We need to talk of the campaign.

SECOND: Ay-men! We must discuss—Macbush!

FIRST: Yes, have that talk, by gosh.

THIRD: You're sure he'll call us soon?

FIRST: (*closing his eyes*): I feel his fingers trembling by the telephone!

SECOND: Let's go! To be back by the time he calls.

THIRD: We'll get a grip on his alleged balls—

FIRST: Yes, fly, and meet me later here for prayer.

(Buzzer sounds)

Now pardon me; I must go on the air.

(SECOND and THIRD exit. FIRST turns toward the audience with a big smile. Black-out.)

ACT I

SCENE 2

(The Palace. Various noblemen clustered downstage. The sound of a helicopter begins, builds, and quits. A red carpet unrolls diagonally downstage from the wing. Trumpet flourish: "Hail to the Chief." Enter KING RONALD down the carpet. Over his dark blue business suit he wears a toy gun-and-holster and a cowboy hat.)

RONALD: I came at once. I want a full report.
Why did you not tell me this news before?

ADVISOR: Sir, when events were in their infancy,
I made to tell you; then someone said, "Not yet—
By the time this thing goes public, he'll forget."

RONALD: Very funny. Then 'tis a tangled web?

ADVISOR: The most, Sir. 'Tis a plot whose twists and turns
Might better fit a labyrinth, or else
a Shakespeare play.
The papers all say 'tis the biggest botch
Of state affairs since we began our watch.
We're in deep trouble.

RONALD: There you go again.
I knew some soldiers like him in the war.
In my own squadron there were those who panicked
In a crunch, and jumped ship, ran for cover—

ADVISOR: You fought not in the War, Sir.

RONALD: Eh? Oh. Right.
'Twas in a movie, then; what's the difference?

(Enter a wounded Marine, full of medals. He salutes snappily.)

What bloody man is that? Can he report
Of this revolting mess, and get it straight?

ADVISOR: That's North, Sire.

RONALD: Aye, and that's south, and yonder east, I asked
His name, man; I've still got my bearings down,
Though the Doubting Thomases don't think so—
What's his name?

ADVISOR: North, Sir. Lieutenant North. This is the man
Who like a good and hardy soldier ran
Your foreign policy.

RONALD: By whose command?

ADVISOR: (*plainly discomfited by the question*):
His own alone, Sire. All signs point to North.

RONALD: Aye, and all compasses. Hail, my brave friend!
Tell to your king your knowledge of this case
As thou dost know it.

NORTH: 'Tis quite simple, Sir.
Last year our spies found out the Ayatollah
Had had a hand in killing our Marines
in Lebanon: Iran supplied the bomb.
But rather than retaliating, we
Just turned our cheek. Although the Mullah's mad,
He's anti-communist, and stands between
The Russians and warm water. He also
decides the fate o'th' U.S. hostages
In Lebanon. Our pollsters told us each
Freed hostage was worth ten victories in the House.
So:
Though 'tis our stated policy not to deal
With terrorists, we sold them weapons.

RONALD: How many?

NORTH: No more than what would fill one railroad car,
Or sixty, depending how you look at it.

RONALD: Sixty?

NORTH: Yes. Sir.—I know how much you want

Each hostage freed. Nobody knows that more
Than me. But then we hit a stumbling block!

RONALD: What's that?

NORTH: The Ayatollah had no money, Sire.
The long Gulf War had drained his treasury.
How could he buy our weapons with no cash?

RONALD: What did you do?

NORTH: 'Twas easy, Sir. We asked
Macbush to huddle with some Saudi shieks.
They raised their oil price, which they'd been holding low—
Then, bingo! OPEC followed suit, and all
The rest—Iranian oil, too, fetched more.
So, to conclude, 'twas all your loyal subjects
At the gas pump and the oil furnaces
Did indirectly give the Ayatollah
The wherewithal to buy our ammo, Sire.

RONALD (*to advisor*): Does this make sense to you?

ADVISOR: No—

NORTH: Sir,
there's more:

RONALD: Go on.

NORTH: For these same weapons, Sir, we charged
The buyer thirty million dollars more
Than what we paid to buy them at the source.
This extra profit someone couriered
To Switzerland, where what's left of the guard
Of the hated Anastasio Somoza
Has a Christmas Club account—and there we made
Deposits, though this violates your laws.

RONALD: Oh valiant cousin! Worthy gentleman!

NORTH: I thank you, Sire, and mark, King Ronald, mark:
No sooner had the contras been thus armed—
These Nicaraguan freedom fighters, they

With furbish'd arms and new supplies of men
Began a fresh assault. They burned four schools,
O'er ran a coffee farm, gang-raped a nurse,
And castrated a Delegate of the Word.

RONALD: How they remind me of our Founding Fathers!

(*NORTH etc. all nod.*)

RONALD: And knew all this my right hand man, Macbush?

ALL: Did he, or did he not? That is the question!

NORTH: If I say sooth, I must report he was
Informed—he keeps his own men down there, Sir:
Some veterans of the Bay of Pigs affair.
The day our triumph comes against the Reds,
'Tis sure Macbush will bathe in reeking wounds
To rub some bloody honor on his shirt!
But, Sir,
I tell too much; my own case cries for help.

RONALD: So well thy words become thee as thy wounds;
You are a national hero.
Go: get him an attorney.

(*Exit NORTH and AIDE. Enter ROYAL SPOKESMAN.*)
Who comes here?

ADVISOR: Your royal mouthpiece, Sire. Mark how he speaks—

ROYAL SPOKESMAN: God save the King!

ADVISOR: Whence camest thou, worthy friend?

ROYAL SPOKESMAN (*breathlessly*) From downstairs, Sire:
The newsmen—tv, radio, and print—
Are piled in the pressroom, each one poised
To send some damning story o'er the wire,
To fan our people's ire against us, Sir.
What used to be a still, complacent pool
Is now a froth where these bloodthirsty sharks
Feed on gossip, speculation, outright lies!
MacSchultz himself, that most disloyal traitor,

Began a dismal speech that, lapp'd in proof,
With point by point comparisons, disowns
All knowledge, all responsibility!
Your majesty, our six-year honeymoon
Has ended, and our soiled sheets are hung out
In the daylight, likened to the dirty tricks
That felled the House of Richard twelve years back.
So, to conclude, I've told them to expect
A speech from you tonight. 'Tis only you
Can pacify them with your honey'd words,
Your best grandfather act. Go charm them, Sir.

RONALD: I'll see it done. I'll tell them I knew nothing.
Brash young lieutenants gambled while I slept.
Mistakes were made, yet we're still standing tall!
The slings and arrows shot at me will wound
Th'American people, who cannot bear
To see another Presidency destroyed
With so much left to do: a missile treaty,
A balanced budget, Star Wars, school prayer,
The opening of the dungeon door in darkest
Nicaragua! Come on; let's go write that speech.

(*Exit RONALD and several aides.*)

ROYAL SPOKESMAN: The buck stops here.

ADVISOR: He'll meet it with a grin.

ROYAL SPOKESMAN: What he may lose, noble Macbush could win.

(*All exit.*)

ACT I

SCENE THREE

(*A hotel room. MACBUSH is pacing, reading the WASHINGTON POST.*)

MACBUSH: So foul and fair a day I have not seen.
Something is rotten in the state, and yet
What issue will this come to?
Either I profit from King Ronald's plight
Or else his taint rubs off on me. Events
will show tomorrow what is dark today.
How this affects my cause, I cannot say.

(*Enter an AIDE.*)

AIDE: Macbush, My Lord, Vice-President—

MACBUSH: What is your tidings?

AIDE: Sir, here are the reports you asked for.

MACBUSH: Thanks.

(*AIDE hands him a colorful page of USA TODAY.*)

AIDE: Will that be all, Sir?

MACBUSH: Yes, but stay close by.

(*Exit AIDE. MACBUSH seals door; puts down report.*)

MACBUSH: Now mark this man. His every word's respectful,
Solicitous, most helpful, to the point,
Showing he's hitched his wagon to my star.
Yet all my power's potential. All we do
Is pace around an office worth as much
As a bucket of warm spit. Until the day
When old King Ronald quits, or lies brain-dead,
We are reduced to dedicating ships,
Attending coronations, funerals,
Or waiting on the tarmac, in the rain,
for th'arrival of some pipsqueak potentate
Who has yet more brute power to command
Than I! Oh, I am privy to state secrets;
We breathe each other's atoms in the huddle.
But secondhand, vicariously, I feel
The rush of power—as when, in Druid days,
The high priest ate the God-blessed mushroom, then
Allowed the lesser priests to drink his piss,

That they might feel the copy of his bliss!
And this obsequious servant at my door—
He waits, as well, to feed on what I drop,
Signs on for my campaign, yet he would quit
In an instant if Macbush should plummet
In the polls. Ha! Or maybe he'd remain
And spy here for some other candidate.
In politics there's no one you can trust
Except yourself. And there my problem lies:
My honor, manhood, derring-do—my *self*
Is a mirage caught in King Ronald's glare.
The closer you look, the less there is to see.
Enough! I'll pour a drink, and watch TV.

ACT I

SCENE FOUR

(The same. MACBUSH *turns on TV. He settles into a deep easy chair, back to the audience, thus removed from the scene. Either a live program—projected via camera elsewhere on the stage—appears on his hotel-room TV screen, or a giant cut-out of a screen descends, framing the actors within.* FIRST TELEVANGELIST *enters and faces TV camera. Behind him are eight inflatable plastic women in stylish wigs cradling telephones which are constantly ringing at random. One woman is alive and speaking into her phone.)*

FIRST TELEVANGELIST: My friends, it's not too late. Jesus accepts
whoever stumbles toward him in the dark.
Are you broke down, or tired of your old self?
Don't wait another minute: grab that phone!
Climb out of your dark hole of crime, of drugs,
Illicit sex or leftist politics,

Compulsive self-abuse. You name it: we
Have got the cure! Pick up the phone and dial.
This week when you call us and make your pledge,
You'll join the greatest family in God's country.
Your check will feed one freedom fighter down
In Nicaragua. Fifteen dollars buys
A zip-loc bag of candy, cigarettes,
Deodorant, a Bible, chewing gum,
And a laminated personal greeting card
From you! Our telephones are ringing now!
Don't let that dark totalitarian
Dungeon door swing shut in Nicaragua.
God loves you, Brother. Sister, make that call!

(*Buzzer sounds. Show goes* OFF THE AIR. *Camera rolls off.* TV *screen in* MACBUSH's *room goes dark. Scene remains in* TV *studio.* MACBUSH *remains in chair, not part of the following scene.*)

FIRST TELEVANGELIST: Any calls?

WOMAN: No, Sir.

(*Enter the two other* TELEVANGELISTS.)

FIRST: Where have you been, Friends?

SECOND: In Miami.

FIRST: And how's the weather there?

THIRD: The sailor's wife has chestnuts in her lap.

SECOND: Uh, we can drop the spy-talk now.
Ain't no one listenin' but the Man Upstairs.

FIRST: Yes, tell me your news plain.

THIRD: All right. The attaché we safely stowed
In a Knight of Malta diplomatic pouch
At Southern Air Transport's V.I.P. lounge,
where 'tis guarded 'round the clock by an anti-Castro
Libyan Danish mercenary loaned
by Pinochet, and smuggled to us by
Th' Israeli Secret Service. There it rests

Till the next flight to Tegucigalpa, or
Till we send further instructions. This done,
We took a speedboat ride on Biscayne Bay,
For a first-hand look at the refugee camps.
On every island now marinas bloom,
Studded with yachts, and condos fenced with wire,
Electric gates, and vapor lights, and dogs.
All streets, all mailboxes, have Spanish names!
We sat on the wharf. Then one by one they drove
Up in their Mercedes to tell their tales.
They are the saddest of all refugees—
As Russia, arm in arm with Satan, grabs
For power in the Americas, they flee
To the last great hope of humankind on earth.
Their lives are empty here: far from their homes,
The men play golf, the women watch TV
and money-raise—one gave me this to sell.

(*He produces a large bag of something.*)

FIRST: How sad that those who toil in freedom's fight
Are forced to earn hard cash by wheedling widows
By phone, or cocaine-dealing in the streets.
We warned those creeps in Congress: if you outlaw
Our legal fund-raising for the contra,
'Twill happen in back alleys, like abortions
Before Roe vs. Wade!

SECOND AND THIRD: Brother!

FIRST: Sorry.

(*All bow down and pray.*)

FIRST: You brought the catalogues of this month's market?

THIRD: We have, and we perused them as we flew.

(*He hands FIRST TELEVANGELIST A catalogue.*)

FIRST: Ah, yes. . . . (*Reads.*) STRATEGIC WEAPONS CLEARINGHOUSE.
"Manufacturers' Over-runs of Missiles . . .

Carpenter's Hammers, U.S. Army approved,
Were eighty dollars, now $6.95.
Irregular Grenades As Is. All Tanks
In Stock Reduced Fifty Per Cent, Refused
By Pentagon . . . Slight Imperfections in
Laser Tracking Won't Affect Performance. . . ."

THIRD: (*Reads.*) Israeli Surplus Jets, Helicopters,
Some Assembly Required." Here's one we liked:
"Dear client, you may already have won
This mobile land-based anti-missile system,
Yours for just two million dollars, shipping
And handling, or free if you can trade
One hostage, living, from the following countries,
See chart below for current market values."
Here, try this:

FIRST: What is it?

THIRD: It's a nerve-gas scratch-and-sniff.

(*They all sniff, then freeze in postures of agony. At this instant, MACBUSH's hand in dim light reaches from his armchair and dials the phone. The TV studio phone rings. The THREE MINISTERS unfreeze. Lights come up on MACBUSH. His easy chair turns so the audience can see his face.*)

SECOND: The Phone! The Phone! Macbush doth come!

FIRST: (*putting away catalogue*): More of this anon.

(*While the phone rings, the three join hands and circle three times counter-clockwise.*)

FIRST: Peace! The charm's wound up!
(*to female assistant*): Answer the phone.

WOMAN: Hello. God bless you. Hallelujah. Yes.
(*Aside*): Sir— 'tis he. Vice-President Macbush!

FIRST: Put him on hold. Play Muzak in his ear.

WOMAN (*imitating taped message*): Our operators all are now engaged.

Please hang on till the next available . . . (*her voice fades.*)

(*She hands him the phone. He covers the mouthpiece with his hand.*)

FIRST: He's come to us because he's learned what we
Have known for months: he's lost without our blessing.

SECOND: Without our moral vision for America.

THIRD: Without our money and our mailing list!

FIRST (*into phone*): Speak friend, your wanderings are at an end.
How's that? (*to the others, cupping phone*): He's waffling. This
phone's a weak connection.
Let's activate our satellite uplink.
Access our private transponder,
And beam ourselves into his hotel room!

(*Various mysterious electronic noises.* MACBUSH'*s hotel TV springs to life with a puff of smoke and a bang, and Fourth-of-July sparkler shower. The* THREE TELEVANGELISTS *are there again, on stage and on his monitor, with smoke around them.* MACBUSH, *who has fallen from his chair, is crouching, gesturing agitatedly with his remote control. Enter* MACBUSH'S AIDE, *unseen, responding to the noises.*)

THREE TELEVANGELISTS: All hail, Macbush! Restate your question, please!

MACBUSH: (*overcoming his fear*):
You speak each day with God. Tell me one thing:
Who next shall wear the crown o'th' Teflon King?

FIRST: All hail Macbush! Front-runner! Nominee!

SECOND: All hail Macbush! Vice-President thou art!

THIRD: All hail, Macbush! That shall be President!

ALL: All hail, Macbush, that shall be President!

(MACBUSH, *groping for his chair, falls to the floor.*)

AIDE: My Lord, Macbush, get up! Don't recoil from
The prize you've sought since you were born.
(*to the departing phantasms on the TV screen*): Wait, stay!

(*They stop and listen to him.*)
Is this some special show? My master here
You greet with present grace and great predictions
Of noble having and such royal hope
That he sits speechless here. But tell to me:
If you can look at hats tossed in the ring
And say whose will be trampled, whose will soar
Above the rest—or look at wedding guests
And tell who'll catch the flowers flung, then say:
If he's the next big enchilada, what
Becomes of me?

FIRST: Hail!

SECOND: Hail!

THIRD: Hail!

(*The THREE look at each other in a moment of perplexity. They huddle, then break from the huddle.*)

FIRST: Poorer than Macbush, yet richer.

SECOND: Limited immunity!

THIRD: Only the lightest prison sentence!

FIRST: A fat book contract!

SECOND: A million-dollar advance!

THIRD: Excerpts in *Time, Newsweek,* and *U.S. News!*

FIRST: Thou shalt live like a king, though thou be none—

SECOND: All hail!

THIRD: All hail!

ALL: All hail, the both of you! Amen!

(*They begin a slow fade. They exit, but their image freezes and shimmers on the TV screen.*)

MACBUSH: Don't go! There's so much more I want to know!
How shall this be accomplished? Tell me which
O'th' fifty states are solid in my camp.

What fellow party-members should I fear?
Does Ronald like me still, or does he mean
To cast me off? Shall I speak out now on
The issues? Shall I let the tiger, no,
The pit bull in me out? What opinions
Should I have? Wait! Stay! How can I prove
My manhood? Can I count on your support?
How can you speak right out of my TV
With such prophetic, happy news of me?
Don't go!

(*The picture wobbles, then fades out.*)

AIDE: They're off the air.

MACBUSH: So real, and now
The signal's gone. They're vanished into air.
Into thin air. Would they had stayed, or else
I wish we'd taped them on the VCR.

AIDE: Did we both see that, Sir, or are we both
Too tired, overworked?

MACBUSH: You will be rich.

AIDE: You will be king!

MACBUSH: But when, I wonder, how? They did not say.
You can't trust all they tell ya on TV.

(*Knock on door. They freeze; then AIDE opens door.*)
(*Enter two of KING RONALD's lesser courtiers.*)

FIRST COURTIER: Worthy Macbush, King Ronald hath received
The highlights of your public pronouncements
On this Iran-Contra affair. He knows
Your *personal* interest in the contra cause.
His praises and his warnings do contend
Which should come first. Therefore silence is all
He sends. And like he told the rest of us,
He finds thee holding firm, not breaking ranks;
We all admit mistakes were made, no more.

SECOND COURTIER: We're sent to give thee from King Ronald, thanks,
And an invite to tomorrow's luncheon meeting.

FIRST COURTIER: And for an hors d'oeuvres of your feast-to-be,
He bade me call you, from him, "Nominee."

AIDE (*aside*): What the hell? Is what we just saw true?

MACBUSH: But: there's no convention yet! No caucuses,
No primaries. We've many worthy men.
Why dress me in a suit that's not yet sewn?
Or slip me into boots still being stitched?

(*MACBUSH and AIDE step aside to converse.*)

AIDE: Perhaps it was a joke, sir. You're front-runner.
That you desire the crown, 'tis no great news.
The columnists all say, 'tis yours to lose.

MACBUSH: The nominee! Macbush the nominee!
You heard him! Can't you taste the riches pledged
To you by those who called me "nominee?"

AIDE: It's true. 'Tis strange. Yet it could be a trick.

MACBUSH: Yeah, how do we know a TV preachers's not
A soft-tongued, blue-eyed devil in disguise,
Beckoning us to some most wretched fate?

AIDE: —Or an agent trying to catch us in some sting,
A set-up, like they used before to catch
Those congressmen. . . . (*He steps aside.*)
Cousins, a word with you.

MACBUSH (*aside*): Front-runner! Nominee!
(*To the COURTIERS*):

My friends,
I thank you. Gentlemen, I thank you all!
(*Aside*): These supernatural predictions must
Be right or wrong. If wrong, why do they seem
To start out right? But if they're right, why do

They give me funny chills, make my heart pound
Like when I'm jogging, or like the thrill you get
From doing some illegal, private act?
I've wished for all these spirits did predict;
Now that wish turns to fear,
And horrible imaginings—aha!
My thoughts are murderous, fanatical;
My manhood pulses, throbs, yet it could cease
To function, smothered by the prize it sought:
Then nothing would be there but what-is-not!

FIRST COURTIER: What's on his mind?

AIDE: Oh, nothing.
Nothing, Sir.

MACBUSH: (*aside*): If luck should make me President right now,
I could ease up, relax, not run so hard. . . .

SECOND COURTIER: Macbush can't budge. This honor makes him stiff
Like legs squeezed into Levis not yet washed.

MACBUSH (*aside*): The nominee, he said. I must relax,
Feel good about myself, just let it happen. . . .

FIRST COURTIER: Worthy Macbush, we're waiting for your word.

MACBUSH: Sorry. Yes, tell King Ronald I'll come soon.

(*TWO COURTIERS bow and exit.*)

MACBUSH: So be it!

AIDE: How is't, my noble Lord?

MACBUSH: It's wonderful!
I'm quite wound up. Touching this vision here, (*indicating TV*)
As you are a good soldier, scholar, friend,
Give me one poor request.

AIDE: What is't, my Lord? I will.

MACBUSH: Never make known what we saw on TV.

AIDE: My Lord, I will not.

MACBUSH (*grabbing him by lapels*): Nay, but swear it!

AIDE: I swear!
Honest, I won't, I swear . . . I won't. I swear.

MACBUSH: Think upon what hath chanc'd, and later on,
With more perspective, maybe, let us speak
Our free hearts to each other.

AIDE: It's a deal.

MACBUSH (*suddenly officious*): What were we doing?

AIDE: Looking at reports.

(*They huddle over the* USA TODAY.)

My Lord, this is a random sample of
Opinion on the street, the marketplace,
The towns, by which the people's mind you can
Perceive. The question asked here was, "How do
You rate Macbush? Favorable, or Un-?
Check one description here above, or none."

MACBUSH: Tell me what adjectives or nouns they used.

AIDE: "Vibrant, articulate, strong candidate."

MACBUSH (*liking the sound*): Yes—

AIDE: Six per cent checked that one, Sir, you see
The little yellow bar here on the left.
Across the page is "shrill, unkingly, wimp—"
That's the red bar, fifty-four per cent.
Degrees between are orange, or is that pink . . .

MACBUSH: (*waving him away.*): Thank you.

AIDE: Yes, Sir. (*Exit.*)

MACBUSH (*to the audience*): Here are some cold, hard facts.
I am the front-runner, they say, yet so
Unpopular I cannot *win* the crown!

MACBUSH

I haven't won a vote in twenty years.
I've studied at King Ronald's feet, how he
Enters, as if just finishing a laugh.
He grins, he winks; his every move says, "See:
I'm one of you, yet bigger, happier."
I've aped his gestures, tried to drop my voice
An octave, hung around with football stars,
But nothing's changed. I haven't struck a chord
Among the people. Now rumors say they want
To shut me out of the succession. Well,
I've heard it's lonely at the top: I say
It's far more lonely being so close—one step,
One breath, one heartbeat from the throne—
Yet stuck here like some mountaineer frozen
Just underneath the summit.
It's not my fault my progress halted here.
I've sworn devotion to the king; I've pledged
To bury my opinions 'neath his own.
And he has lasted in his office far
Beyond all expectations. Neither guns,
Nor old age, scandals, deficits, nor his
Bad jokes have done him in. For all he knows,
This world's a silver screen where you can be
Shot full of holes and still come back to wave
Behind the credits and the music—
It's not my fault I'm not a movie star,
I've never tumbled with a starlet, I
Have yet to cuddle with a chimpanzee
Or fight a duel with capguns. I'm a man!
A real man! Scratch me, and I bleed! And yet,
The paradox is: *I* must prove *my* manhood!
Front-runner! Nominee! Now let Macbush
Prove, am I made of metal, or of mush!

(Exit MACBUSH. *The door and jamb shake. The TV, still glowing, gives forth a puff of smoke.*)

ACT I

SCENE FIVE

(The Palace. Various nobles clustered. Trumpets without: "Hail to the Chief." Sound of helicopter rises and diminishes. KING RONALD enters in a World War I leather flight jacket.)

RONALD: Has North been disappeared? Where are the ones
I named to my commission? Their report
You must digest for me. Where is Macbush,
My right-hand man? It's time we had a talk.

AIDE: Sir, North is gone. He's left his office quicker
Than a union leader in El Salvador.
His attaché he took; his shredder died
A brutal death. I spoke with one who saw
Him leave, who said that frankly he confessed
His reasons, although publicly he'll claim
The Nuremberg Defense.

RONALD: Where is he now?

AIDE: He's desaparecido, Sir. Either
He's meeting with his secret team, or else
He's moving on to other things—
Some say he's organizing break-ins in
Church basements, law rooms, opposition homes,
Or drawing up macabre scenarios
For instituting martial law. I fear
His patriotic zeal may hurt you, Sir—
He loves this land not wisely, but too well.

RONALD: I'll take no part, of course,
To plan the man's obstruction of this case.
He is a man in whom I placed great trust.
Is all now ready for my speech?

AIDE: Yes, Sir.

(*Enter MACBUSH and his AIDE. RONALD notices them.*)

RONALD (*speaking into microphone, which is not turned on*):
Worthy Macbush, the best vice-president
I ever have a recollection of!

(*The microphone is turned on. RONALD does not notice.*)

Your servile speeches, preaching my gospel,
Your blind praise of our voodoo economics
Have shown your lap-dog loyalty—(*He notices*)—What? Damn!
Is this thing turned on?

(*He turns it off.*)

Sorry, just a joke!
Macbush, for your support, we owe you much.
Our right-wing crowd needs your patrician touch.

MACBUSH: The service and the loyalty I owe,
In doing it, pays itself. Your highness's part
Is to receive our duties. I would not
Be standing where I am, were't not for you.
(*Aside*): Why has he called me here?

RONALD: You're like a seed I've planted in the soil
Of our great nation. I have watered you
And bathed you in my light. I've watched you grow
In your office. Yon seat is meant for you.
While I am speaking, let all subjects see
My constellation's other stars, whose glow
Will light our skies for years to come. Excuse me.

(*KING RONALD moves off.*)

MACBUSH: My moment's come. The king looks old. Mark how
He wanders, unconnected to the present.
His plenteous love for me, that hid itself
Before beneath his macho public self
Now gushes out. I'm sure he means to pack
It in, to hand his crown, his throne, to me
Before his legal term expires. He knows
Annointing me ensures his programs will

Survive—preserved by my incumbency!
I'm free at last. I feel my manhood surge
While his is softened, and that gland that rules
Virility in him is swollen, sick:
He'll steer his ship of state into the harbor,
Retire to his ranch in Santa Barbara.

(*KING RONALD returns, with LORD MACDOLE and LORD KEMPF. They sit in chairs near MACBUSH, who also sits, and eyes them uneasily. The THREE EVANGELISTS also enter, behind. They exchange a knowing wink with MACBUSH. He relaxes.*)

RONALD (*at the microphone*): My friends, my fellow citizens, lend me
Your ears. You working people, moms and pops,
You true heroes, you common building blocks
Of our uncommon nation—and these men
Behind me here, whose names we cannot speak
Without we put an "Honorable" before:
I come to praise America, not to say
I'm sorry. There's no wrong in what we've done.
Evil men and their bad news make headlines;
Good news is oft interr'd on some back page.
That gets me in my keister. Newspapers
Have told you our men broke the law—a vicious
Attack, but if it's true, it's all my fault:
Straightforwardly will Ronald answer it.
Here, right in front of Macbush and the rest—
For Macbush is an honorable man,
So are they all, all honorable men,
Come I to tell you I am still in charge.
Our men in uniform are proud today:
We've rolled the Red Tide back all o'er the globe. (*Applause.*)
Inflation's down, and unemployment, too! (*Applause.*)
Though we've two hundred billions of red ink,
The coffers of our generals are full! (*Applause.*)
Though, this, in fact, seems parardoxical. (*Applause.*)
When that the poor have cried, Congress hath wept!
Lawmakers should be made of sterner stuff.
Yet they are all, all Honorable men.

Nay-sayers claim we fan the flames of war:
You all did see last year in Rekjavik
I thrice presented their king our peace plan,
Which he did thrice refuse. Was this aggressive?
I'm here to say our country's standing tall,
And none are taller in it than these three:
The great Macbush, the Lords of Kempf and Dole.
Now I am old. My kingly days will soon
Be done. All cares, all royal business I
Will drop, and let them fall to younger strengths.
You know my crown and throne do carry me
Above the fray of party politics.
My fellow citizens, were I to stir
Your hearts and minds to choose one nominee.
I should do Macbush wrong, Lord Kempf, Lord Dole,
Who, you all know, are honorable men.
I will not do them wrong, but only say
We will establish our estate upon
One of these three—or someone else—whoever
Doth seem the noblest to you, the big star,
The most deserving. Good night. God bless you all.

(*Applause.*)

(*NOBLES all rise, chatting and shaking hands. The THREE TELEVANGELISTS come downstage, conferring, noticed only by MACBUSH and his aide. The FIRST TELEVANGELIST hangs back a little from his two partners.*)

THIRD TELEVANGELIST: Come, Brother, we have much to do.

SECOND TELEVANGELIST: We must raise funds for "country number two."

FIRST TELEVANGELIST: Go, then, I'll join you presently . . .

(*He eyes MACBUSH across the stage. MACBUSH eyes him.*)

Mark with what sugar'd fervor Ronald speaks,
And says "or someone else." "Or someone else."
Why not? They say the next king must command

The TV camera: he alone will win
Who broadcasts the most power, comfort, calm,
With a sawdust preacher's most persuasive voice . . .
Then why not me? There's no one—not even
Ronald himself—more at home on the tube.
Beware Macbush, in my mind's eye I see
The hand of God in the first primary.

(*FIRST TELEVANGELIST exits, stopping to touch MACBUSH's shoulder, as in laying-on of hands. MACBUSH is deep in thought.*)

RONALD: Macbush, to lunch! I have some news for you.

MACBUSH: Anon, Sir. (*RONALD exits, with others.*)

AIDE: This pensive frown ill suits you, Sir; they'll say,
"Yon Macbush hath a lean and hungry look!
He thinks too much: such men are dangerous."

MACBUSH: You're right. (*He re-arranges himself.*)
There's just so much to keep in mind.
Go. Get the car.

AIDE: Yes, Sir.

(*The two LORDS KEMPF and DOLE, who have been standing aside, cross MACBUSH's path. All three tip their hats and briefly touch their toy guns-and-holsters. Exit KEMPF and DOLE.*)

MACBUSH: Lord Kempf, Lord Dole,
He said, or someone else. They are all steps
On which I must fall down, or else o'erleap,
For in my way they lie.

(*MACBUSH has wandered over to the rostrum, feeling its majesty. He speaks dreamily into the microphone.*)

(*Amplified*): My dear fellow
Americans, it is with heavy heart . . .

(*He notices the microphone is still on. He jabs his finger at the switch.*)

Out, Microphones! And spotlights, dim your fires! (*The lights dim.*)
Let no one hear, or see, my black and deep desires!

(*Exit* MACBUSH. *Blackout.*)

ACT II
☆☆☆☆☆

SCENE ONE

(The castle of MACBUSH *at Kenn O'Bunk. New England seacoast sounds: foghorn, waves on rocks, seagulls barking. In her kitchen,* LADY MACBUSH *is cutting a chicken. She stops to read, again, a letter from her apron pocket.)*

LADY MACBUSH (*reads*): ". . . and I'm sure they must have supernatural knowledge. When I said, wait, tell me some more, they went off the air. Just blackout. We were standing there scratching our heads when in walked two of King Ronald's men, who called me "Nominee." I'm not kidding. Just the way the Three Weird Brothers said it. I just had to tell you. It's really exciting. Don't tell anyone.
I'll see you Friday. . . ."
Macbush, thou art the President-to-be.
I feel it. Yet I fear to watch you snatch
Defeat out of the jaws of victory.
If there's something in your path, you'll trip on it,
Or swerve and lose your way. You would be great,
Ambitious, yes, but with no instinct for
The jugular. What you most want you must
Win—by yourself, without these holy men.
Macbush, you want the thing that hollers out
"To win me you have got to tell the world
What you believe and what you feel!" How else
D'you get the multitudes to bear your banner?
Who else but you can tell 'em where you stand?
Come home; we'll have a talk; I'll spill into
Your ear some woman's sense. If you can dare
To let your feelings out, we may get rid
Of all that's kept you so far from the throne,
The crown, which Fate and evangelical aid
Do seem about to thrust on you, withal.

(Enter a HOUSE SERVANT. *Whenever a door opens in the Palace at Kenn O'Bunk we hear the sound of gulls.)*

LADY MACBUSH: What's up?

SERVANT: The King comes here tomorrow, Ma'am.

LADY MACBUSH: Really? And what's the reason for his trip?

SERVANT: He comes at Lord Macbush's invitation
To take the ocean air.

LADY MACBUSH: And where's your boss,
My husband, Lord Macbush, when I need him
To help me with the preparations?

SERVANT: Ma'am,
He said he'd be here soon, but first he had
Some business in the capital. If I
Said more, I would invent his message.

LADY MACBUSH: You bring great news. Thank you!

(*Exit SERVANT. As he exits, brief sound of seagulls and surf. A coarse cry of triumph escapes from LADY MACBUSH's lips.*)

The gulls
Themselves are hoarse that croak the fatal entrance
Of old King Ronald to our summerhouse!
Come, you spirits that wait for mortal minds
To give you birth and life; come, fill me up
With direst cruelty—wait, wait a minute:
What? What's come over me? Was I about
To think a wicked thought? To give a speech
Whose every word dripped blood —as if some poet
Of bygone times ghost-wrote my lines for me,
And filled my lips with words whose only purpose
Was to show the evil, bitchy woman lurking
Behind th'ambitious man? To lay the blame
For *his* remorseless acts, his dirty tricks,
Upon my woman's breasts! Blame the wife? Wrong!
'Tis here
The parallels 'twixt ours and other tales
Must bend—my generation has outgrown
The stereotype of the bloodthirsty wife.
Macbush, you and your muttering ministers,

Wherever, out of sight of us,
They plot their latest mischief; who came, last night,
And called thee from the smoke of hell, hear me:
That my knife stabs only here in the kitchen;
I'll not creep through the blanket of the dark . . .
I'll make your speeches, go to teas, I'll take
Your hand at the convention, but no more.
Do what you will, but take the blame yourself!

(*She goes on cutting and chopping. Sea and gull sounds up, then fade out.*)

ACT II

SCENE TWO

(*Foggy Bottom. A region near the national capital. Night-time. An imposing building's entranceway. An inflatable Marine guard guards the entrance. Lights come up on* MACBUSH, *getting out of a limo. His* AIDE *is driving.*)

MACBUSH (*to his Aide*): Wait for me here.

AIDE: Yes, sir.

(*The Author of the play enters. He snaps his fingers;* MACBUSH *and the* AIDE/DRIVER *freeze.*)

AUTHOR (*to the audience*): I hear you turning pages.
Keep still your hands. It is no use: you'd search
In vain for this scene in your script, or in
That ancient book our story seems to copy.
These next few lines you will not find in print:
This part was censored by the hoary spies
Who read all books, all articles that would
Expose the secret stuff that goes on here.

This next scene made them nervous; it destroyed
Their curtain of deniability—
They ripped three pages from the text somewhere
Between Act Two, Scene One, and old King Ron's
Arrival at Macbush's door. It could
Be worse: they still could burst in here upon
The stage, and clap their hands on th' actors' mouths.
They could rip up all
The baseless fabric of this vision,
The hotel room, the king's palace, this set—
Tear it down and leave an empty stage behind.
This is such stuff
As prison sentences are made of—
I beg your pardon for this detour, Folks,
Anon we'll get back to the famous scenes:
To Kenn O'Bunk, the seagulls and the surf.
One errand still awaits. Macbush, awake!

(*Exit Author.*)

(MACBUSH *comes to life. He shakes his head, rubs his brow nervously.*)

MACBUSH (*to AIDE*): Wait here.

AIDE: Yes, Sir.

(MACBUSH *pulls out a flashlight and shines it at the doorway.*)

MACBUSH: This is the Agency of Spies itself.
Encyclopedias could well be writ
About the darkest doings done within
These granite walls. A history
Of all the mischief crafted in this place
Would shock to speechlessness the most devout
Aficionado of Hollywood horror films.
I ought to know. I used to run this place.
But that's all by the way. There is a man
I need to talk to here—a scientist
Skilled in the alchemies of poisons, of
Illegal substances, of shellfish toxins,
Of viruses, nerve gas, and alkaloids

That alter the highest functions of the brain.
I mean to ask his help.

(*He inserts a punch-card into an imaginary slot. A synthesizer plays the first bars of "God Bless America."*)

(*Enter* SCIENTIST.)

SCIENTIST: Macbush! It's been a while. Have you come back
To reminisce about old times? What plot
Delights most in retelling? The cigar
We tried to poison for the Cuban prince?
The stuff in Santiago? The toothpaste tube?
The airplane engine, stalled ten thousand feet
Above the plains of Africa? Or (*he whispers in* MACBUSH's *ear*) bzzz?

(*They both laugh.*)

MACBUSH: Where can we talk? Is this place bugged?

SCIENTIST: Of course!
But come, I know a room wherein the din
Of garbage compactors and shredders will
Drown out our words—

MACBUSH (*to audience, apologetically*): This is the censored part!

(*The* SCIENTIST *mimes opening a door. Immediately the theatre is filled with the noise of machinery.* MACBUSH *and* SCIENTIST *pretend to speak over the din. The* SCIENTIST *shuts the door. Light fades on them. Noise stops*)

(AIDE, *who has frozen aside downstage—holding a steering wheel to suggest limousine—comes to life. He puts down the wheel, gets out of car, leans against car, lights cigarette, addresses audience.*)

AIDE: Did you ever wonder 'bout the folks you work for?
You take a man who's been in training to
Be King since he was six years old—a man
With a big edge: his birth, his resumé,
His current job, his name a household word,
His features known to all: and still he wants

To play with a stacked deck, t'enlist the help
Of God and his three vicars, and now this—
This sleazy agency that roams the world,
Helping to power the motliest assortment
Of fascists, yahoos, Moonies, Jesus Freaks,
Demented colonels, and gold-hungry goons
Of every size and shape—This agency
Now boards Macbush's bandwagon.
And if what happens now *I* hear or see,
Then *I* am part of the conspiracy. . . .

(He stubs out cigarette and exits as MACBUSH *and* SCIENTIST *return.)*

SCIENTIST: So then, Go home, be merry, look content.
Tomorrow night look that he lie alone.
Let not his guards lie with him in his chamber.
Take then this vial, his being then in bed,
And this distillèd liquor pour into
His lips, from which through all his veins shall run
A cold and drowsy humor; nothing but pulse
Shall keep his native progress, all else ceased.
No harm will come to him; he will but sleep.
No warmth, no voice, shall testify he lives:
His red cheeks will be pale like ashes, and
His footlights will fade out, his curtain fall,
As in a theatre, when a bad review
Shuts down a play and sends the actors back
Into the street, to th'unemployment line,
Leaving only stagehands, electricians
To say there was a drama in this place!
Then each part of our fumbling government—
Th'executive, the legislative, too—
Shall, stiff and stark and cold, appear like death,
Till, as the manner of our country is,
Yon population in the morning comes
To rouse you from your bed, proclaim you King,
And in your best suit and spit-polished shoes,
Thou shalt be borne by helicopter to

The Palace, leaving thus your present eclipse!
—*If* no inconstant toy nor womanish fear
Abate your valor in doing what I say.

MACBUSH: Give me! Give me! Oh tell me not of fear!

SCIENTIST: Hold! Get you gone! And when you've prospered thus,
I'd hap'ly be the Agency's new boss.

(*Exit SCIENTIST, back through the guarded entranceway.*)

MACBUSH: Aide!

AIDE (*returning*): Sir!

MACBUSH: Have we been seen?

AIDE: By no one, Sir;
That is, but for the moon, whose wat'ry eye
Sees all, or yon Marine, who hath not twitched
One muscle, or (indicating audience) all these folk here, who paid
Coin of the realm to watch this plot unfold.
They're theatre junkies, Sir: your secret's safe
With them. Glued to their seats, they wait to see
What next emotion—wonder, terror, woe—
Will buzz or startle them. Where to?

MACBUSH: The airport.
Whether this next test I will pass or flunk
'Twill all be clear tomorrow in Kenn O'Bunk.

(*Exit MACBUSH and AIDE. Re-enter SCIENTIST.*)

SCIENTIST: In case you're wondering, folks, whether this play
Has taken an irrevocably violent turn,
Relax: we called it "comedy"—remember?
The bottle's filled with water—H_2O—
And a drop of Red Dye Number Two; however,
The end result may be the same. Sick people
Are often cured by a placebo. Rats
In laboratory experiments bear out
The *expectations* of their researchers.

Whether King Ronald's eyelids can resist
Macbush's power of suggestion, well,
'Tis yet too close to call. I plan to read
About it in the papers.

Exit SCIENTIST. Fade to black.)

ACT II

SCENE THREE

Kenn O'Bunk. Helicopter noise, wind across stage. The Helicopter sound fades, replaced by foghorns, surf, buoy bells, and gulls. Flourish of trumpets. Enter KING RONALD and attendants.

RONALD: This castle hath a pleasant air. The view
Nimbly and sweetly recommends itself
Upon our senses. Yet 'tis chillier
Than Malibu. But what a place! Macbush
Was to the manor born, I guess, and so
Was his old lady.

(*Enter LADY MACBUSH*)

LADY MACBUSH: King Ronald!

RONALD (*briefly imitating Bert Parks*): There she is!

LADY MACBUSH: You're welcome in this house, Sire; let the light
And briney air relax your weary mind
And give you strength as long ago it did
The paralytic King at Campobello.

RONALD: I thank you for your trouble.

LADY MACBUSH: All our service

Is but poor thanking for those honors deep
You laid upon our house, when you didst choose
Macbush Vice-President!

RONALD: And where is he?
Out on the campaign trail? Or meeting with
His secret friends to plot the latest move
Against the threat of third world revolutions?

LADY MACBUSH: He's just arrived.

RONALD: Show me the way. Conduct me where he be.
He likes to hear me call him "Nominee."

(*LADY MACBUSH starts off. KING RONALD and his chief of staff stand on the doorstep. Gull sounds cut off.*)

CHIEF OF STAFF: I-I don't like this. Something's making me
Nervous. It's quiet—too quiet—out there.
Like in the forest when the birds and squirrels
Do cease their chirping when the wolf pads by;
Like Main Street in El Paso just before
The sheriff and the bad guy shoot it out.

RONALD: Nonsense!
There's not a breath of danger in this scene.
And if there was, so what? Who can avoid
An end that's purposed by the mighty gods?
What says our daily horoscope?

CHIEF OF STAFF (*consulting book*): "Relax . . .
Someone close to you shares your responsibilities.
You are about to take a long vacation."

RONALD: Ya see? What did I tell you? Let's go in.

(*Both exit. Gulls. Waves.*)

ACT II

SCENE FOUR

(Kenn O'Bunk. Interior. A library/study. A wall of fake books, a TV, a Hide-a-Bed. A window view of the sea. Various servers are seen passing back and forth to the dining room. MACBUSH *is pacing. He is wearing faded imitation-Western style clothes.)*

MACBUSH: If only I could do the deed right now,
And, doing it, have done with everything:
Know in that moment how *to be king* feels,
To be the be-all and the end-all once
And then to die, to quit the earth, knowing
That reverence and honor would be paid
To the memory of me. But it's no use:
Reality is here, and I am in it.
I fear the complications of this plot—
How it could backfire. I wish that I
Were man enough to win this prize without
Resorting to what some would call a crime.
I know the judgment here: even before
The jury's out, even before the deed
Is done, the simplest verdict is to send
The ingredients of this child-proof bottle
Down my own throat, send me to sleep—to sleep,
Perchance to dream: aye, that's the easier way,
For in that death-like sleep what dreams may come—
The fantasies of my whole life! I can't
Go on. He is my king, and now my guest.
He's popular. He's made this nation great
Again. If I should send him riding off
Into the sunset, to thunderous applause,
His hoofbeats' dust will choke me. I've no spurs
To kick my gutless horse here in the side.
Only ambition! Damn!—and what I heard
Those ministers on television say.

If I could tune them in again, hear their
Advice once more, or borrow some of their
Technique, their savoir faire . . ..

(*TV does not come on. He slaps it.*)

This damn TV!

(*He picks up the phone.*)

What was their number? 1-800-J . . .

(*Enter LADY MACBUSH. She touches his shoulder. He jumps, surprised, puts down the phone.*)

LADY MACBUSH: The King has almost finished his lobster.
Why do you dally out here in the hall?

MACBUSH: He's asked for me?

LADY MACBUSH: Of course! It's your home, your own dining room.
The place is full of satisfying sounds
Of lobsters being cracked and sucked, while yours
Lies pink, unviolated, on the plate!
Your clams, that steamed themselves agape, go cold
While you deny to warm them with your lips.

MACBUSH (*Aside*): We will proceed no further in this business.
He's called me "Nominee." Then why not bask
A while in glory and expectation,
Not risk it all so soon!

LADY MACBUSH: What's this old junk
In which you dressed yourself? You slept in it?
Where is my old Macbush, my dear; art thou
Afeared to be what all are calling you?
Are you a coward, a bloodless vegetable
Hoping some holy wizards on TV
Will tell you your next move?

MACBUSH: No! Of course not!
I dare do all that may become a man.

LADY MACBUSH: You must do more! You want to be *The Man.*

MACBUSH: If I should lose?

LADY MACBUSH: You lose. You lose. Let not
Your fear of losing keep you from the race.
Dig in your Nikes at the starting place
And you won't lose. When King Ronald has supp'd,
We will with wine and muzak so relax him;
Talk to him then; persuade him a long rest
Would do him good—the country needs your youth—

(*She whispers the rest in his ear. Exit LADY MACBUSH.*)

MACBUSH (*removing medicine bottle from his pocket*):
She's right: the King is old, and so stone-deaf,
He cannot hear the nation's call for bold,
Young leadership—we lurch through crises: AIDS,
The stock market, the hostages, the judge
The Congress ate up and spat out, the wars
In oil fields and tropical jungles,
While he but grins and draws vacation pay.
How long the King will sleep, she does not know—
False heart must hide what false face cannot show.

(*Exit MACBUSH. As he exits, the TV finally comes to life. The three TELEVANGELISTS are on the screen. A sweet hymn is playing.*)

FIRST TELEVANGELIST: My friends, the greatest joy this side of Heaven
Awaits you now. The ecstasy of writing
Checks. You know your donations are all we have
As weapons in the war with Satan's forces.
I don't have to tell ya—we've had hard times
With scandals, lust, dissension in our ranks.
Our theme park is a ghost town now, except
For the tent where people pay to see our doghouse!

(*Enter LADY MACBUSH. She sits and watches, drawn to the TV, gradually becoming mesmerized.*)

Meanwhile the contra teen-agers are idle;
The funds for their assaults have been cut off;
With their last few quarters they play video games
Like SWAT and JUNGLE WAR to keep their trigger
Fingers sharp—yes, more than ever now we need
Your hard-earned cash: you should see our lawyer bills!
We've come so far; don't let your amigos down.
And look to the East where hordes of howling Persians
Do lust to shed your blood: can anyone doubt
A Mighty Tribulation comes! And only those
Who are with us will be saved. The rest are lost!

(*TV fades; LADY MACBUSH in blue afterglow. Fade to black.*)

ACT II

SCENE FIVE

(*The same. Much later. The house is dark. Enter* MACBUSH'S AIDE, *in pajamas, holding a flashlight. He is tipsy. He is speaking in two distinct voices, reciting Shakespeare from his memory of a college course.*)

AIDE (*as older man*): How goes the night, boy?

AIDE (*as boy*): The moon is down.

AIDE (*as older man*): . . . And she goes down at twelve.

AIDE (*as boy*): Aye, 'tis later, Sir.

AIDE (*as older man*): Here, take my sword;
A heavy bladder lies like lead upon me,
So that I could not sleep.

(*Enter* MACBUSH, observing)

AIDE (*still in boy's voice*): My Lord, you still awake? (*Realizes, coughs*)

AIDE (*in his natural voice*): My Lord, Macbush, you still awake?

MACBUSH (*nods nervously*): You, too?

AIDE: Yes, Sir. Er, I've been thinking of those three
Wizards we saw on the hotel TV.
To you they've showed some truth.

MACBUSH: And to you too,
They will someday. Till then, best be like me.
I have not thought of them one moment, nor
Given any heed to what they said.
Important men like me have more to do.
Yet, when we both should find a moment free
Let's talk again about their prophecy.

AIDE: Sir, where's—

MACBUSH: Upstairs. The first door on the left.

AIDE: Good night.

MACBUSH: Good night. (*A clock begins to chime.*)
Go. Go, get thee to bed.

(*Chime continues. MACBUSH takes vial out of pocket.*)

Is this a bottle which I see before me,
Its label toward my hand?—Come, let me clutch thee.
I close my eyes, and yet I see thee still.
Am I sure it's not a vision sensible
To feeling as to sight? A false creation,
Proceeding from my night-oppressed brain?

(*Clock continues to chime.*)

No, I see it still. It draws me on.
I go, and it is done; the bell invites me.
But hear it not, my King; it is a chime
That marks the hour you ruled for the last time.

(*Chime reaches twelve; stops.*)

(*Exit* MACBUSH. *Enter* KING RONALD, *in an enormous child's sleeper, carrying teddy bear, or a monkey-toy, wearing a crown over his cowboy hat, and his toy holster and cap-gun.* KING RONALD *paces the room nervously. He gazes out the dark window. He sits on the couch.*)

KING RONALD: How many thousands of my poorest subjects
Are at this hour asleep! Oh, Sleep, how have
I scared you off, that you no longer come
To steep my old brain in forgetfulness?
Why do you go instead, to give relief
To convicts in the most filth-ridden jails,
To Salvadoran rebels crouched in holes
Beneath night skies aglow with tracer fire?
Sleep! Why d'you come to peasants brushing flies
Away, and yet no longer snuggle in
The perfumed master bed of state, where I
Lie sated with seafood, wine, and salt air?
Why close the eyes of the homeless, unwed mother
Cradling her infant on the subway grate,
And not tuck me in on my kingly couch?
Sleep! Do you visit weary teen-agers
Twisted in tiny compact cars' back seats
With punk rock blaring on the ghetto box,
And the strain of safe sex engraved on their brows—
And in the calmest and most drowsy night
With all appliances and means to boot,
Deny to help a king? Oh, Mister Sandman,
Then let your magic silica shower down;
Uneasy lies the head that wears the crown!

(*Enter* MACBUSH.)

MACBUSH (*Aside*):
He lay not in his chamber, I— (*Sees* KING.)
My Lord,
What, still not sleeping?

KING RONALD: No.

MACBUSH (*Aside*): You see?
His eye is hollow, and he looks quite changed.

(*KING RONALD beckons MACBUSH to sit beside him on the couch. MACBUSH agitatedly does so.*)

KING RONALD: You know, Macbush, by what strange, crooked ways
I won this crown: my Western movie days,
My midlife philosophic switch, my years
Selling refrigerators on TV,
And then the secret group I formed, to sow
Unrest among the people, to steal the notes
To my opponent's speeches, and to strike
The deal with those old Mullahs in the East
Not to release their hostages while yet
My predecessor ruled. While I've been king,
I've taught my people to feel good about
Themselves . . . Now all my reign
Hath been a fiction, like a magic kingdom
That families visit, or like a comic film
That audiences flock to, forgetting
The storm outside, their empty pocketbooks—
We nearly disproved that old platitude,
"You can't fool all the people all the time."
When they awoke to budget deficits,
To poverty, star wars, and acid rain,
I sought to distract all the nay-sayers
With foreign quarrels. I
Invaded a defenseless tropic isle,
I exercised our Navy, and bank-rolled
Three continents' worth of counter-revolutions,
Trained armies and police around the globe,
And all the while no crisis left me sleepless:
Even when missiles flew, and our jet fighters
Engaged our enemies, my own advisors
Never woke me up. But now all's changed; the force
Of my obsession tuckers out; I reel
From one new setback to another, whether
In congress or the stock market. The thrill
Is gone. I try to rally my scattered troops,
But lack the zeal to pass the programs we've

All yearned for, and what's more, now I can't sleep.
At meetings I don't recognize my staff—

MACBUSH: Great King, let's open up the Hide-A-Bed. (*They do it.*)
Sir—if you please—I have a potion guaranteed
To give you sleep: a family remedy.

KING RONALD: I wish mine eyes would shut, and my thoughts, too,
As they are so inclined . . .

MACBUSH: Please, Sir, do not
Omit this offer. 'Twill be a comfort, Sir.

KING RONALD: Thank you, Macbush; you ever were most loyal—
(*hesitating*) It's not illegal?

MACBUSH: No!

KING RONALD: It won't show up
In my weekly urine test tomorrow?

MACBUSH: No.

KING RONALD: Is this the "Just Say No" stuff?

MACBUSH: No. No. No!
Just drink it, Sire, and I myself will guard
Your person while you rest, and watch your safety.

KING RONALD: Thank you. (*drinks.*) Wondrous heavy . . .
(*He removes his crown.*) Set me the crown upon the pillow here.

(*MACBUSH does so.*)

(*KING removes his holster.*)

My weapon, too. (*MACBUSH places it.*)
So tired. Good night.

MACBUSH: Sleep tight.

(*KING RONALD appears to sleep. Slowly MACBUSH reaches*

over, takes holster, puts it on, admires it, draws the cap-gun, takes crown, tries it on.)

MACBUSH: Come on, you turbann'd Persian, you Russian bear,
You sleazy Nicaraguan commie, draw—
You face a brand new marshall at High Noon!
Drop to your knees, and whine on, harvest moon!
Sleep well, Americans; Macbush keeps watch—

(*KING RONALD awakes.*)

KING RONALD: What, ho? My crown!

MACBUSH (*scared*): Sir, right here—I was just,
Uh, buffing it, and stowing it up here.

KING RONALD: (*incoherently*):
Macbush, . . . the evidence, . . . drug running flights—
The palace, . . . right-hand drawer . . . I do forget—
No one must see the document . . . marked . . . (*He sleeps.*)

MACBUSH: Sir, please! He sleeps. Not to awaken till
Weeks hence, divorcéd from th'imperial crown.
His last few words hint something that may trip
Us up—but later! Now put the free world's strength
Into one manly arm! Nothing shall force
This lineal honor from me—mine, from him;
Mine by succession, what I could not win!

(*Exit MACBUSH. KING RONALD sleeps, snores. Clock chimes "One." Sound of knocking at the door. Sea gull sounds rise and fade.*)

(*Black-Out*)

ACT III

☆☆☆☆☆

(SOUND EFFECTS OFF: Confused shouts, voices, calling at random: "The King is dead!" "Awake!" "Awake!" Sound of sirens, alarm bells. "What!" "Ho!" "Help!" Sirens, human wailing, feet running, automobile tire screeching, engine noises, helicopter. "What?" "No?" "Asleep?" "He won't awaken?" More bells, alarms, teletype. Music: "Hail to the Chief." Teletype, newscaster voice, ". . . and that's the way it is . . ." Static. Trumpets.)

PROLOGUE

(Outside the palace. Winter. Night. A HOMELESS MAN has lit a fire in a large tin can. Enter a HOMELESS WOMAN.)

HOMELESS MAN: Who's there?

HOMELESS WOMAN: Nay, answer me. Stand and unfold yourself.

(HOMELESS MAN stands and opens his blanket, letting her in. They wrap and warm themselves together.)

WOMAN: For this relief, much thanks.
'Tis bitter cold, and I am sick at heart.

MAN: You fled the shelter, too?

WOMAN: Aye, that I did.
With roaches, fleas, drug pushers, and the shrieks
Of madmen just de-institutionalized,
I thought I'd find more comfort in the street.

(They rest and warm themselves.)

MAN: You'd think that having a new king would be
A sign of luck to us—I've heard it said
In the old days with the changing of the guard
There was great celebration: jails were sprung,
Oxen were roasted for the poor; fresh kegs

Of ale were tapped on street corners, orphans
Got gift certificates at Bloomingdale's . . .

WOMAN: Aye, not too many calendars have shed
Their pages since that new king, Jimmy Who,
invited all the poor draft dodgers back
With open arms.

MAN: Aye, th' only amnesty
Macbush hath ordered is a pardon for
All those found guilty in the contra mess.

WOMAN: And as for food and clothes and medicines—
For every dollar's worth he flings to us,
There's twenty million sent to fund the rebels
In Honduras, Mozambique, Afghanistan.

MAN: —While full one-quarter of the world is starving.
What the rich throw out, we all could live on:
If they would yield a small percent of their
Excess, 'twould be a living for us, but
They like, I think, to see us lean and hungry.
It makes them sure of their abundance; my words
Are strong, yet I speak just in hunger
For bread, not in thirst for revenge.

WOMAN: Well, things may change. Th'election's coming up.
Macbush may try to win some liberal votes
By showing off his sympathetic side.

MAN: 'Tis also true he's been pre-occupied.
It's taken all his narrow intellect
And that of his moronic chief-of-staff
To sink the Central American Peace Plan
Without appearing to, and then to sign
A treaty with the Russians, just enough
To satisfy th'electorate, without
Halting the arms race one iota.

WOMAN: And he's still getting o'er the shock of his
Painful succession. I heard someone say
For weeks while Ronald slept, they brought him out

To meetings, state functions, and propped him up
And no one knew the difference—that it took
Two months to find a government doctor who
Would swear he hadn't always been like that,
Would swear he was unfit to lead the nation.
It was some acupuncturist; they paid
His malpractice insurance premium
For the next ten years, they say . . .

MAN: And did you hear
When old King Ron was finally carried out,
They found six closets full of cowboy boots
And crates of Clairol hair dye, and—

WOMAN: And did
You hear that when Macbush put on the crown,
It fell down past his brow and scratched his nose?

(*While joking thus, the two homeless people rise and move on in the night.*)

MAN: You know, there's murmurings afoot . . .

(*Fade to inaudible. Light fade to black.*)

ACT III

SCENE ONE

The Palace. The throne room. Enter Macbush's chief Aide.

AIDE (*imitating the weird ministers*):
"All hail, Macbush, now in our glass we see
Vice-President, and President-to-be!"
You've got it all now—the whole package deal
The three weird preachers promised, yet I fear

You played not by the rules o'th' game—and yet
Methinks I'll not divulge my doubts until
I figure how to hasten the good luck
They did predict to me. If all their words
Are true—as you, Macbush, have proved so far—
I stand to cash in, too, when the time's right.
But hush! Here comes my boss, Macbush, the King,
To toss his new-found hat into the ring.
No sooner has he copped the crown and throne,
But the presidential prim'ries have begun!

(*AIDE busies himself, arranging desk, holding chair back for* MACBUSH. *Enter* MACBUSH, *agitated, and cronies carrying mounds of paper. Enter TV tech crew.*)

MACBUSH: What do you mean, there is no evidence?

CRONY (*whispering*): I tell you, Sir, we've broken into all
Th' offices on this list. Your revenue
Police have audited the tax returns
Of every left-wing 501(c)(3)!
It's all honest—there's no conspiracy!

MACBUSH: So it's just a plain coincidence that millions
Of duped Americans line up to turn
This country over to the Communists
Without us firing a shot? To think
Some punk in green fatigues and sunglasses
Is brainwashing the ladies of our church
Auxiliaries, convincing them that he's
A Patrick Henry clone—it makes me mad!
Go, get him on the phone! And ask him if
He's man enough to meet me face to face.
Whatever—tennis, golf, a yachting race,
Or tiddlywinks—let 'im name the time and place!

(MACBUSH *sits at throne/desk.* AIDE *adjusts his tie and crown.* ATTENDANTS *gather to give applause. Camera whirrs and dollies in.*)

VOICE: On camera, sir.

MACBUSH: Good evening.
My fellow citizens, you all recall
With what surprise and what a heavy heart
I took this seat from which I speak tonight
To you—to all of you. We all did love
King Ronald hugely, and none more than me.
To him I owed the opportunity
To know the honor, the excitement of
My duties as assistant King, a job
So swell, I would have been content to keep it
Forever, if God had seen fit to let
King Ronald drink some cocktail from Olympus,
So he might reign immortal: we all agree
There never was a greater King—he did
Bestride this narrow world like a cowboy
On a huge stallion, and the rest of us
Walked under his big legs and peeped about
To follow in his hoofprints. He did cure
Our great malaise, and had us standing tall
In no time flat—a beacon bright of hope
To the oppressed, a source of terror to
Our enemies, who gained not one square inch
Of turf while Ronald manned the battlements! (*Applause.*)
Now as your King, I ask your loyalty, too.
As you did love King Ronald, love me, do.
And if you want to see his best ideas,
The dreams he couldn't quite nail down, fulfilled,
Then let me be your candidate: Macbush,
Your King, your President, and Nominee! (*Applause, and chanting: "Four more years!"*)
And one more word: to all our enemies
Out there—I know you're listening, whether
By spying satellite, or cruising in
Your "fishing boats" offshore, or skulking in
Our public libraries—and to my foes
Who stand more near to hand, to all of you!
You know America's been led by men
Of iron since we sent the redcoats packing.
We breed a race of leaders here—real men,

Not grey-faced technocrats, or bow-tied wimps,
Or Wellesley graduates in cardigans
And circle pins. Eyeball to eyeball, we
Will never blink. It's my turn now. You flexed
Your muscles, beat your chest, but could not push
King Ronald back. Nor will you budge Macbush.

(*Applause.*)

Thank you. Thank you. God bless you, and good night.

(*Music: "Hail to the Chief."* MACBUSH, AIDE, *cronies and reporters move off.*)

ACT III

SCENE TWO

(*The same. Seeing the space now emptied, two courtiers return:* LORD MACDOLE *and* LORD KEMPF, *both holstered and riding hobby horses, which they constantly pet and whisper to, as if to calm their fiery spirits.*)

LORD KEMPF: Did you hear that? "My foes more near to hand?"

LORD MACDOLE: I did. And did you mark, "With heavy heart
I took the throne!" Heard you the flattery
And mourning he would heap on our old King?

KEMPF: What will you do? Let us not hang around.
To show an unfelt loyalty's a strain
False men can manage easier than we.

MACDOLE: You know, this Big Sleep that laid Ronald out
May yet be hov'ring here. It may condense

Again like some mysterious yellow rain
And zip up our eyes, too, till none of us
Is left to thwart Macbush's ambition.

KEMPF: Aye.
The nearer we stand, the nearer 'tis to danger.

(*Enter, of a sudden,* MACBUSH.)

MACBUSH: Lord Kempf, and you MacDole, I looked for you
Without. You're both invited to our house.

(*MACDOLE and KEMPF regard each other. Their horses pace.*)

MACDOLE: Your Highness, thank you, but we must beg off.

KEMPF: We'll take a rain check, please.

MACBUSH: You're leaving town?

MACDOLE: Aye, my good lord, it is that time of year
We ride a-horseback through our bailiwicks
To sound the minds of our constituents.

MACBUSH: I would have liked to hear your good advice
In this day's meetings. Are you riding far?

KEMPF: I go, my lord, to the much-disparaged city
On yon Great Lake—the home of chicken wings.

MACDOLE: And I to the cornfields whence Dorothy flew
To Oz.

MACBUSH: I trust you'll both be back to steer
My legislative package through the Congress?

KEMPF: We will, my lord. As fast as hobby horse
Can fly.

MACDOLE: Go not our steeds the better, we'll
Ride in as the Speaker's gavel strikes the board.

MACBUSH: Fail not, and listen as you ride:
We hear our opposition is entrenched
In New England and Iowa, spreading rumors.

BOTH K. & D: Rumors, Sire?

MACBUSH: Aye, Rumors touching our incumbency—
The strange condition of King Ronald, too.

KEMPF (*aside*): Aye, what a sleep was this for your advance
ment!

MACBUSH: Aye, rumors, harmless jibes—our rivals here
Are dwarves; there's no real man among them,
None fit to *hold* this palace! If they stopped
Their mousey scurrying one moment, and
Stood perched upon each other's shoulders, they
Could still not peek into the window here!

(*They all laugh. Helicopter sound begins. Trumpet flourish.*)

My chopper revs; I hear the trumpets toot.
So, ciao; I wish your horses swift of foot.

(*Exit MACBUSH. Helicopter sound builds and fades out. LORDS KEMPF and MCDOLE watch it fly away.*)

KEMPF: What were we saying? Some quite unpleasant sound,
As of a dog's shrill yapping for attention,
Did interrupt my thoughts—

MACDOLE: —Our present fears—

KEMPF: Ah, yes. This narrow-necked Macbush.
Strutting and crowing his hour upon the roost,
Proclaiming "I'm a man" to a doubting world,
May try to prove it by taking a peck
At you or me.

MACDOLE: Let us away. We'll ride
The country round, seek out the few outposts
Of our false King's support, and neutralize 'em.

KEMPF: Therefore to horse! Our safest course is to
Avoid the capital, and let's not stand
Too long and watch the clock.

(*They draw near to discuss their plans.*)

Now, I'll fake left
And run a wide sweep to the right.

MACDOLE: Okay,
And I'll go long straight down the middle.

KEMPF: Right.
Find out how deep the opposition is.

MACDOLE: What will you do?

KEMPF: I'll start a speaking tour,
Go autograph my book at shopping malls.

MACDOLE: You wrote a book? An economics text?

KEMPF: The story of my life. It's called "Mein Kempf."
Fare well! Let's keep in touch. (*LORD KEMPF rides off.*)

MACDOLE: We'll both away—to see how we
Can pull the rug out from Macbush together.
And then, when that is done, we face each other:

(*Exit MACDOLE, riding. He returns in an instant to say*):

—or someone else! Hy-yo, away!

(*Exit MACDOLE.*)

ACT III

SCENE THREE

(*Kenn O'Bunk. Sound of Seagulls, surf, bell buoy. MACBUSH in his library, throwing darts at a photograph of Daniel Ortega. MACBUSH is nervous and downcast.*)

MACBUSH: Now I am King. But to be King is nothing
If still I don't feel safe. My fears run deep,
Especially of Lord Kempf and MacDole.
They both command some following, both are known

For "leadership"—I can't rest easy while
They're free to run against me. I—
(*knock without*)
Who's there?

AIDE (*enters and bows on one knee*): Good morning, Sire. Here are the news reports—

MACBUSH: Get up! I want the news, man, the bad news;
Don't plead for mercy till I hear it.

AIDE: Sir,
Your third-world debt repayment plan has hit
A snag.

MACBUSH: What plan was that?

AIDE: You know, the one
Where we ship out our toxic waste and pay
Some busted country cash to take it in—
Then they have money to meet their monthly payments
To Citicorp and Chase Manhattan, Sire.

MACBUSH: What a neat plan!

AIDE: It cost us nothing, too:
We raised the cash to pay 'em by selling bonds—Hazardous
Waste Notes—The *Wall Street Journal* said
They were the best paper that Uncle Sam
Had sold in years, and people flocked to buy them!

MACBUSH: I know: the toxic stock syndrome. So what's
The snag?

AIDE: There's been a revolution on
The island of St. Angina, Sir; two ships,
Two freighters full of waste have been turned back
From the port. They were about to dump it there

For landfill for a luxury resort.
It's on its way back to New Jersey now.

MACBUSH: Send down some spies, a fifth column; we'll see
How long it takes t'upset their applecart!

AIDE: Uh, yesterday
The Senate voted ninety-eight to two
To form a new bi-partisan committee
To watchdog your spy agency, my lord.

MACBUSH: Go on.

AIDE: Yes, Sir: The Central American Peace Plan—
That's theirs, not ours—has garnered the support
Of six more countries, and the D.A.R.
It's just us and the Afrikaaners now.

MACBUSH: But what about the Contras? We can't turn
Our backs and walk away from them. They need
A homeland!

AIDE: Yes, Sir. We took a poll. Their choices were
Fort Lauderdale or Southern Idaho.

MACBUSH: Dear God—what else?

AIDE: There's been a plane crash, Sire.
Our air traffic control's a hopeless mess.
A Jumbo Jet. 'Twas full of industrialists
From Singapore, Korea, and Japan,
Bound for your Eastern-Seaboard
Surplus-Skyscraper-Buyout-Auction-Sale.

MACBUSH: Were there survivors?

AIDE: No. And, Sir—

MACBUSH: There's more?

AIDE: Aye, two more hostages taken in Beirut.
That brings it to a total of twenty-three.

MACBUSH: And what's their current value on the street?

AIDE: (*looking at table*): Ten million, Sire, in gold or Japanese bonds.
Or th' equivalent in merchandise, you know.

MACBUSH: And did you call our broker yet?

AIDE: Yes, Sir.
He thinks it's not quite time to buy. He says
The market's soft; the price is going down.

MACBUSH: Is that all?

AIDE: No, Sir. A full page ad appeared
In twenty major dailies yesterday,
Signed by eight hundred scientists who've refused
All Star Wars research work; they're led by that
Old Nobel physicist, claims SDI
Will never work.

MACBUSH: Throw physics to the dogs,
I'll none of it! It's got to work! It's our
Last hope! Is nothing going our way?

AIDE: Not much, Sire.
There's a move afoot to bring King Ronald back,
Whether or not he sleeps. And here is yet
Another writer asking why you've not
Yet chosen a vice-president—

MACBUSH: Enough!
Now go; stay outside till I call.

AIDE: Yes, Sir. (*Exit AIDE.*)

MACBUSH: The world is too much with me now. My country
Loves me not: even my home town is against me.
Sometimes I wish I'd kept a drop o'th' stuff
I gave King Ronald, enough for one night's sleep—
Sleep that knits up the ravel'd sleeve of care—
Last night I tossed and turned. I thought I heard
A seagull crying, "Sleep no more, Macbush;
Macbush hath murdered sleep!" I never knew
How much there was to worry about, as King.

Until the last, King Ronald never seemed
Pre-occupied. I'd love to ride around
Like those two guys, Lord Kempf and Lord MacDole,
Stop at a watering place, knock back a few,
Tell jokes, go home and tumble with the wife—
Then sleep!

(MACBUSH *picks up a Penthouse Magazine, scans it, absorbed.*)

There is a divinity that shapes her end!

(*Enter* LADY MACBUSH. *He hides the magazine.*)

LADY MACBUSH: How now, my Lord, why do you keep
Alone, thinking your sorry thoughts? Are you
Still worrying about your manhood, or
Regretting the uncertain way you won
The throne? Why think on it? What's done is done.

MACBUSH: My manhood's fine, just fine, don't put it down.
As for the other. . . .
(*Aside*): We've only charmed the snake, not killed it—
If we but turn our backs, it may wake up
And sink its poison fangs into our foot.

(*To* LADY MACBUSH *again—like a TV commercial*):

This headache, nightmares, and my sinuses—
Who needs this job? If only some reporter
Had tracked me to a townhouse with some bimbo,
Or found I'd cheated on a law school test,
Or smoked some of that Texas loco-weed,
I'd be disqualified now—I could sleep
Far from the pacing guards, the telephones
Poised humming by my head, about to jar
The night's peace with some new emergency!
King Ronald's in *his* bed; he's sleeping well,
Where nothing ill—no harried messenger,
No hijacking, no flock of geese on radar,
Nor low-intensity war heating up,
Can interrupt his rest.

LADY MACBUSH: Come on, my dear;

You do unbend your noble strength, to think
Like this: sleek o'er your rugged, manly looks;
Be bright and jovial on the news tonight.

MACBUSH: Oh, full of scorpions is my mind, dear wife.
You know that Lords MacDole and Kempf still prowl
The countryside, stirring the people up.

LADY MACBUSH: What of it? You are holding all the cards.
You're President—your mighty office gives
The upper hand to you.

MACBUSH: That's true, they are
Assailable. Then rest assured, dear wife,
Before too long, I will announce some news
To stop them in their tracks.

LADY MACBUSH: What do you mean?

MACBUSH: Let it surprise you, too, my sweet, then you
Can join the general cheering. Go, get me
A soda water, please.

(*Exit LADY MACBUSH.*)

What ho, my Aide?

(*Enter AIDE—almost too quickly.*)

AIDE: You called me, Sir?

MACBUSH (*writing*): I did. Go, take this note
To whom it is addressed.

AIDE: Yes, Sir. (*Exits.*)

(*Enter LADY MACBUSH.*)

LADY MACBUSH: My dear,
Your mineral water . . .

Macbush (*staring over bubbles*): I have this . . . deja vu, you know:
Like every line I speak
Were but an echo of some speech I've heard
Before—perhaps on Masterpiece Theatre?

As if some satirist wrote my lines for me,
Or some poor hack on Saturday Night Live.
And yet I lack direction, I'm unsure
O' th' blocking—I stumble, and bump into things.
Tomorrow I will contact those three fellows
I saw on television. They're the ones
Who stirred me up, and now I need to know
What my next move should be. I'm like a plane
That's low on gas halfway across the sea:
To turn around would be more risky than
To stay on course, hoping to make the coast . . .
I am the pilot now; my door is locked
And all the rest are passengers, all strapped
Into their seats, helpless and wondering
How steady are the hands on the controls.

LADY MACBUSH (*from doorway*): My dear, it's time for bed.

MACBUSH: Yes, come; we'll go to bed.

(*He steals a last look at the magazine. Aside*): My self-abuse
Is just a symptom that we want hard use.
We are yet young indeed! (*Both exit.*)

ACT III

SCENE FOUR

(*TV Board Room again. Clock strikes eleven. Thunder. Enter the three TELEVANGELISTS in raincoats. As they shed umbrellas and macs, the phone rings.*)

FIRST TELEVANGELIST: Hello? God bless you! Hallelujah—
Oh!
(*Holding hand over phone*):
Damn! I mean darn! It's God! And is He pissed!

THIRD TELEVANGELIST: How do we know it's God?

FIRST TELEVANGELIST: I recognize His voice.

THIRD TELEVANGELIST: Well, push the button;
Make it a conference call.

SECOND TELEVANGELIST (*fearfully*): What did we do?

FIRST: Uh, Lord, you sound ticked off; uh, what's the scoop?

GOD: (*As voice booming over executive phone*):
Have I not reason, brothers, haven't you
Now gone too far? How did you dare
To trade and traffic with Macbush
In riddles and affairs of state;
And I, your Maker, your Father and
Your Mother both, you didn't call
To ask Me My opinion!

(*The THREE MINISTERS quake, and try to conceal themselves under desks, etc.*)

You never call Me anymore!
—So wrapped up as you are
In the gaudy trappings of this sinful world,
Thinking not how far you wander from the truth!
What's worse, this politician whom you help
Is a wayward one who, you must see
Works for himself alone, and not for Me!
But make amends now: get you gone,
And meet Me in the morn, when he
Will come again to know his destiny.
Think also to provide the means
To wipe your own sorry slates clean,
And leave your bodyguards at home.
I'm signing off now—I alone
Can straighten out what you've begun.
Meanwhile I'll draw Macbush along
In his confusion. He'll spurn fate,
Scorn good advice, and raise his own
Obsessions high above all public wisdom,

Like every King before him.
You all know national security
Has ever been the truth's worst enemy!

(*Angelic trumpets sound over the phone.*)

And mark this: nowhere in My scriptures—
Neither the ones engraved in stone,
Nor on the scrolls unearth'd in caves,
Wilt thou find that I instruction gave,
To you or others of your cloth,
To raise money for counter-revolution!

(*Angelic trumpets sound again.*)

Therefore prepare t'accept the punishment
I'll plan for you as fits your crime!

(*Trumpets sound.*)

Hark! I am called. My little sidekicks three,
Go now to Foggy Bottom, and wait for Me!

(*Amplified click and dial tone.*)

THIRD TELEVANGELIST: Come, let's make haste—

SECOND TELEVANGELIST: Yeah, let's get outa here.
I wonder what He has in store for us?
Wilt come?

FIRST TELEVANGELIST: You go; I'll follow.

(*SECOND and THIRD Exit.*)

I'm not worried:
He sounded angry, but the righteous have
No need to fear God's wrath. Besides, His words
Yield *sometimes* more than one interpretation . . .
I think what most upset Him was: we meddled
In the campaign of a humanist like Macbush.
For this He's made us squirm, and now He waits
To see how guiltily we show ourselves. . . .
Let others quail, retire from politics,
Declare bankruptcy, join a Holy Order . . .

Let others fear a telephone call like this;
I take it as a sign; it all depends
On how you look at it—
If the Greatest Tribulation the world has seen
Is down the road, then one of *us* should take
The driver's seat, so says the Lord.
"Riddle Macbush, to throw him off the scent;
Help me and I'll help you."—that's what He meant.

(*Exit FIRST TELEVANGELIST.*)

ACT III

SCENE FIVE

(*A meeting room, on the campaign trail. Enter* MACDOLE *and* KEMPF.)

KEMPF: Let us seek out some desolate shade, and there
Have a good cry.

MACDOLE: Let's rather give a shout,
And leap into the trenches to defend
Our country. Let us ride the exercycle,
Sweat in the sauna till we're lean and ready.
Each day new sorrows strike our party and
Our people. Farms foreclose, the dollar falls,
Investors shoot their brokers; even the rain
Turns sour, as if the heavens above did taste
America's bitterness, and spat it out.

KEMPF: You know I do believe what I believe,
And mean what I do mean, say what I say:
I say what I mean, think what I believe!

MACDOLE: I know, I know.

KEMPF: I will not be put down without a fight!
This tyrant king whose name blisters our tongues
Has yet to touch us. I am young and vig'rous—
You've been around; this may be your last chance
To strike a deal with him—some cabinet post—
And offer me as sacrificial lamb
To appease an angry god.

MACDOLE: I am not treacherous.

KEMPF: But Macbush is.
See how his treachery doth *trickle down*
Till all of us become a trifle more
Suspicious of each other. Pardon me.
Let's help each other in the primary.
You are who you are, were, ever will be,
And I am, too, and either one of us
Would hold the throne against the Donkey men
Far better than that fraud, Macbush.

MACDOLE (*gazing out window*): I know.
Methinks I almost see their armies gath'ring
On the horizon, their ranks swelled with new
Recruits: blacks, women, homosexuals . . .
They're led by brash young officers whose names
We've barely heard before, their neckties loose
And suitcoats slung over their shoulders like
A badge of relaxation. Meanwhile,
Their two or three most powerful generals
Are holed up in their headquarters, waiting
To see if they should buckle weapons on
And join the fray.

KEMPF: 'Tis plain to see they seek
To resurrect the days of young King Jack,
Their idol, who was murdered in the sixties.

MACDOLE: Alas, Poor Jack—I knew him. Rumors said
Macbird, or Tricky Dick, did have a hand
In his untimely death.

KEMPF: Nothing's been proved,

And any documents that might shed light
On what's still unsolved in the case lie locked
In the palace archives until forty years
Are stacked behind the next millenium!

MACDOLE: And since Macbird retired in disgrace
Their party has been drifting, out of touch
With the mainstream, and out of power, too.

KEMPF: Except for those four years of Jimmy Who—

MACDOLE: A fluke! But there also a lame imcumbent
Was run aground—and well I know; 'twas I
Who sought to blow some wind into his sails:
In vain!

KEMPF: I have no crystal ball, nor pay
Much heed to pundits or prognosticators,
And yet I think we lose this next election
Unless we can dethrone Macbush before.

MACDOLE: And do it in a way that saves the Union,
And casts no shadow on ourselves, or on
Our party.

KEMPF: And we must do it soon, before
Macbush, through deeper mischief, or waging war,
Can make his young incumbency so entrenched,
We can not cut him out—like a small mole
Whose deep and winding roots
Resist the surgeon's knife.

MACDOLE: Have we no friends
Will help us rid the country of this hell?

KEMPF: We do! Look here—while we've been talking, I've
Been making up a list. Each name—

(*Knock on door; KEMPF hides list.*)

Come in!

(*Enter* MACBUSH'S AIDE, *agitatedly.*)

AIDE: My Lords, Macbush the King has sent this note
To you by me—you two may be, my big,
I mean, be mine, maybe, behind, I may—
Behind the high and mighty back, we may—

KEMPF: Good God, man, what's your meaning? If it be
Important to us, let us have it straight!

AIDE: I want to work with you.

KEMPF: For me?

AIDE: For you. For him. For you, the both of you.

MACDOLE: But why? You've been Macbush's flunky since
Before your chin grew whiskers. Why the change?

AIDE: My lord, I love my country more. We need
A leader not infected by the germs
Left by the Iran-arms-drug-running scam;
A king who will not try to prove his manhood
By sacrificing soldiers in some jungle;
A king who's cut no deals with Jesus freaks,
Nor ever worked as head of Sleuths and Spies,
Nor rose to power by some insidious means,
And if that doesn't point to one of you,
Then a Donkey's our next king.
(*Aside*): If they accept, 'twill help my writing, too.

KEMPF: We do agree with you—and here are more
Who'll work to bring the tyrant down.

(*KEMPF shows list.*)

We welcome you, and bid you stay on in
Your service of Macbush; just be our eyes
And ears and nose within the palace. What
You can't smell out, you may spy into. Then—
(*Knock on door.*)

Hold on!

MACDOLE: Who is it?

KEMPF: State your business.

MACDOLE: Speak!

(*He throws open the door. Enter a Senator, another conspirator.*)

KEMPF: It's safe. He's one of us.

SENATOR: Have you two heard the news?

MACDOLE: What news?

KEMPF: No.

MACDOLE: No.
Does it concern us all? Or is it some
More private woe, to make one single heart
Lurch in its chest?

SENATOR: It doth concern the country,
But part of it pertains to you alone.

MACDOLE: To me?

SENATOR: To you.

MACDOLE: Then let me have it—quick!

SENATOR: Your wife—

MACDOLE: Oh, no, my wife—

SENATOR: You do not know?

MACDOLE: No! What?

SENATOR: O cursèd spite! That I should bear
This news!

MACDOLE: My wife! What's happened to my wife?

SENATOR: You haven't heard?

MACDOLE: I said! I haven't heard!

SENATOR: Macbush—

MACDOLE: Macbush?

SENATOR: Macbush hath named your wife Vice-President!

(*MACDOLE slams the table and covers his face.*)

KEMPF: Merciful heaven!
What, man! Ne'er pull your hat upon your brows;
Give anger words! The rage that does not speak
Deposits in the heart, and bids it break!

MACDOLE: My wife?

SENATOR: Your wife.

MACDOLE: My Liddie?

SENATOR: I have said.

KEMPF (*Aside*): She ever was an independent sort.

MACDOLE: My wife? But why? Why did she not refuse?

SENATOR: Would you refuse
To be your hist'ry book's most proud entry:
The first female American V.P.?

MACDOLE: What treachery! Macbush will stop at nothing!
Now he will get the women's vote—

KEMPF (*Embracing him*): Take comfort.
Make of your rage a vitamin, a tonic,
To make you fight the harder.

MACDOLE: He has no shame, no scruples. What, my wife?
My pretty one? (*He breaks down.*)

KEMPF: Dispute it like a man!

MACDOLE: I will do so, but first I have to feel
It like a man! No—like a woman who
Is strengthened by a royal flush of tears.
Did she do this, and never seek my advice?
(*Aside*): Or: does she have some deeper purpose in it?

KEMPF: Be this the whetstone of your sword. Let shock
And wrath convert to action. Go for it!

MACDOLE (*With controlled panting*):
Oh, I will play the woman with my eyes,
Mike Tyson with my fist!—You, there!
House managers and ushers, let them have

An intermission here, but make it quick!
Smoke half a cigarette, but not king-size,
Then crush it quick beneath your heel out on
The street, gulp down your drink, then rush back in:
I'll not wait long! Then bring me front to front
With foul Macbush! Within my pistol's range
Set him, and duck for cover!

(MACDOLE *draws his capgun and fires thrice toward the door, thus completing the previous line's iambic pentameter.*)

KEMPF: Now your tune grows manly, mate.
Come, go we to the King. His note invites us.
Our power is ready, and the world looks on.
Macbush is ripe for shaking on his throne!

(*Exit* MACDOLE, KEMPF, AIDE, SENATOR.)

(*Trumpets sound. Black-out.*)

INTERMISSION

ACT IV

☆☆☆☆☆

SCENE ONE

(Kenn O'Bunk. A dark night. One low light is on in the library. Enter a PSYCHIATRIST and a FEMALE SERVANT.)

DOCTOR: This is the second night I've watched with you.
I don't yet see—

WOMAN: Shhh. Since my lord Macbush
Went on the campaign trail, she hasn't been
Herself. I've seen her—middle of the night—
Get out of bed, throw on her robe, and come
Down here. She turns on the TV, then sits
And stares at the same program, or if that's
Not on, she watches the blank screen. It's like
She's hypnotized, sir; then she opens up
Her pocketbook, takes out her checkbook, and
Starts writing checks, a slew of them, and then
She seals each in an envelope, and licks
The stamps, and then returns to bed. But, sir,
She does this in her sleep!

DOCTOR: That's no surprise.
I have seen many who, while seeming to
Watch the TV, are, in the main, asleep.
And does she speak?

WOMAN: At times.

DOCTOR: What does she say?

WOMAN: I'd rather, sir, you listen, I—Shhh! She comes!

(*Enter LADY MACBUSH with a flashlight.*)

DOCTOR: How came she by that light?

WOMAN: From L. L. Bean.

(*LADY MACBUSH sits and turns on the TV. The THREE TELE-VANGELISTS appear in the midst of a fund drive. The volume is too low to hear.*)

DOCTOR: You see, her eyes are open!

WOMAN: But their sense
Is shut! Now look: she takes her checkbook out—
Shhh.

LADY MACBUSH: God be praised!

DOCTOR: I'll write down what she says, then look tomorrow
For meaning, if indeed any exists . . .

LADY MACBUSH: Here's one. That's not enough? Then here's another.
Fie, my lord: a soldier, and afear'd?
What need we fear, when we hold all the power?
They only fear who do not make donations.

DOCTOR: Do you mark that?

LADY MACBUSH (*poking an imagined corpse with her foot*):
O dainty duck! What dreadful Dole is this?
Is it the senator, or is it Liz?

DOCTOR (*to woman*): We hear what we should not.

WOMAN: She's spoke what she should not! God only knows
What true things feed her fancies!

LADY MACBUSH: Here's a check. Here's another. All doomed . . .
All the oil of Arabia . . . Oooh!

DOCTOR: What a sigh is there. Her heart is sore.

WOMAN: For all I envy her position, I
Would never want such sorrow in my breast.

(*LADY MACBUSH presses her two hands on the television screen. She leans back as if in ecstasy.*)

DOCTOR: This is beyond the scope of my poor practice—
She needs a specialist, a doctor skilled

In deprogramming devotees of cults,
You know, like Bagwan Shree Baksheesh,
or Swami Snatchadollar.

LADY MACBUSH: "Let me help you," he said. "I do resent,"
She said, "your patronizing attitude . . ."

DOCTOR (writing): What does this mean?

LADY MACBUSH: "I cannot say it, but it rhymes with 'rich.' "

WOMAN: It makes no sense.

LADY MACBUSH: To bed, to bed; come, put your p.j.'s on,
And wash your hands—I tell you, he's asleep . . .

(*laughs*)
He'll not come out of his bed . . .
Come, come, come, come,
Give me your hand,
What's done can't be undone! To bed, to bed!

(*LADY MACBUSH stands, pretending she is in an official receiving line. She smiles, shakes DOCTOR's and WOMAN's hand as she goes.*)

LADY MACBUSH: Yes, so nice to meet you, I'm sure . . .

(*Exit LADY MACBUSH.*)

DOCTOR: Will she go now to bed?

WOMAN: Directly, Sir.

DOCTOR: Foul whisperings are abroad. Unnatural deeds
And covert acts will out. Whether by deep throats
In the garage, or sleepwalkers by night,
The truth gets told. Good God, forgive us all!
When apathy and ignorance remove
The vast majority from taking part
In voting and decision-making, then
A small, secretive, treach'rous group
Can run a country for their own ends, can
Wreak their covert havoc o'er the world,
And we only hear by accidental leaks

The lawless moves they've made to keep themselves
In power. Well, look after her. Good night—
My mind she's boggled, and amaz'd my sight.
I think, but dare not speak.

WOMAN: Good night, good doctor.

(Gull sounds rise and fade. Buoy bell, foghorn, fade to black.)

ACT IV

SCENE TWO

Foggy Bottom. A parking garage, just before dawn. From the street below, sounds of passing sirens, occasional truck gear-shifting. Thunder. Eerie, witch-like electronic music. Enter SECOND and THIRD TELEVANGELISTS, stealthily. Sudden sound of tomcats fighting in an alley. Both ministers jump. They are lugging stuffed attaché cases and a large metal trash can.

SECOND TELEVANGELIST: I don't like this place.
How do we know Macbush will come?

THIRD: It's all arranged. God said. Don't question it.

SECOND: And why no bodyguards?

THIRD: You've got the greatest bodyguard of all.
Remember '68: Even that huge
Ex-lineman could not save Prince Bobby K
From the Palestinian assassin's gun . . .

(Loud truck backfire boom. They both jump!)

SECOND: Oh, forgive me my sins!

THIRD: Mercy upon us!

SECOND: Art thou afeard?

THIRD: Be not afeard; this alley's full of noises—
Sounds and foul airs that give offense, but hurt not—
Sometimes a thousand jangling horns will blare
About my ears, and sometimes sirens, that
If anyone within a mile were trying
To sleep, forget it—then, like a nightmare,
I'd think all headlights would flick on, and show
Hoodlums ready to pounce on me, so I
Just stare ahead, and walk, and pray to God.

SECOND: Does anything ever happen?

(*THIRD shakes his head. Loud backfire boom. Both jump!*)

(*Enter FIRST TELEVANGELIST with piles of paper: correspondence, logs, financial statements, news clippings, receipts.*)

THIRD: Did anyone follow you?

FIRST: No. Here. Get this going. 'Tis time.

(*They throw some of the papers into the trashcan and light it. As they pitch more and more documents in, they become mesmerized by the flames, and gradually come to dance around the can, chanting.*)

SECOND: Round about the trashcan go!
In the fire now we throw
Drugged red wine and perfumed pillow,
Naughty preacher's peccadillo.
Hush money and secret payments,
Rival lawyers' warring statements!
Pink Rolls Royce and false eyelash!
Praise the Lord and go first class!

ALL: Trouble, trouble—gospel squabble;
Fire burn and cauldron bubble.

THIRD: Round about we jump and twitch!
In the fire now we pitch
Maps of airstrips on plantations,
Reports by Heritage Foundation;
Phone number of Palace cellar,

Gun of Catholic priest guerilla.
Photos of contra leader's lover,
Request for A.I.D. deep cover—
Soldier of Fortune back issues,
World Anti-Communist League dues,
Names of friendly corporate boards:
Go first class, and Praise the Lord!

ALL: To the flame our flim-flam fizzle;
Fire burn and trashcan sizzle!

FIRST: Round about we whirl and sing!
In the fire now we fling
Textbooks not teaching the Creation,
Pre-millennial dispensation!
Cancers of the world excised,
War against the Antichrist!
True believers' healed afflictions,
Gospel's End-Time dire prediction:
Judgment upon sinful nations—
Great and Final Tribulation:
Armageddon's tidal waves,
Sleepers, awake, and open graves!
In the Beginning was the Word:
"Go first class, and Praise the Lord!"

ALL: Double, triple, quadruple trouble—
Planet burn and oceans bubble!

(*Thunder. Tomcats fighting, loud. Electronic music builds, as they wildly hurl more documents into the rising flames. A sudden silence:*)

FIRST: By the twitching of my thumbs,
Something wicked this way comes.

(*Enter* MACBUSH, *nervously.*)

MACBUSH: How now, you secret, black, and midnight wizards?
What are you up to?

ALL: A deed without a name!

MACBUSH: I order you, as your Commander-in-Chief,

Howe'er you get your knowledge and your power—
Whether by reaping whirlwinds, or by daring
The foulest fiend himself to show his face
Until the whole earth sicken—answer me!
Some things I have to know.

FIRST: Speak.

SECOND: Demand.

THIRD: We'll answer.

FIRST: Uh, tell us first, if you would like to hear
It from our mouths, or from an unnamed source.

(*Pointing upward with his thumb.*)

MACBUSH (impressed): You can do that?

FIRST: Uh, first we have to spice the brew a bit.

(*He adds invisible magic crystals to the fire.*)

FIRST: First pour in blood of AIDS-infested faggot!
And armpit sweat scraped from th'electric chair!

(*The flames flame higher.*)

ALL THREE: Come high or low;
Thyself and deadly office show!

(*FIRST TELEVANGELIST takes out a huge flashlight, throws a shadow of SECOND or THIRD on the wall. Shadow waits on wall for MACBUSH'S first question. The remaining TELEVANGELIST beats the trashcan lid.*)

MACBUSH: Tell me, thou Unknown Power,
How deep is my support? Is my throne safe?
If any—

FIRST: Hush! He knows thy thought. Just listen!

VOICE: Macbush! Macbush! Macbush! Beware MacDole;
Beware Lord Kempf. Beware.

MACBUSH: Aha! Whoever you are, I thank you much.
'Tis but an echo of my former fear.

King Ronald praised them in his speech the same
As me—but wait—

FIRST: He's gone, but here's another, stronger still.

VOICE (*over loud can-lid thunder*): Macbush! Macbush!

MACBUSH: I'm here! Were I plugged into my Walkman,
I'd hear thee.

VOICE: Great Macbush, be resolute
And laugh to scorn at ordinary mortals:
For no man who is whole can hurt Macbush—
Only the man who's not entire can harm thee!

MACBUSH: Then live, MacDole, and Lord Kempf, carry on.
What need I fear thee? Still, just to make sure,
I may dispose of you as best I can.

FIRST: The fire flares again! There's more to hear.

(*The shadow dances wildly. All are transfixed by the dance.*)

VOICE: Be brave, be proud, be free and have no fear
Who runs against you, who comes stalking near!
Macbush's great flagship shall ne'er be sunk
Till burning food doth come to Kenn O'Bunk!

MACBUSH: What means this "burning food?" Wait, tell me more!
It all sounds great, but my heart throbs to know
One thing—

FIRST: Adieu, Macbush, we must depart.

ALL: Seek to know no more . . .

FIRST: I'll see you in New Hampshire.

MACBUSH: Wait! Let me pay you for your information—

SECOND: No money now.

THIRD: You are a charter member
Of our club; we'll bill you monthly—

FIRST: And if at any time you want to cancel—

(*All three exit laughing loud. Flames flicker. Weird electronic music.*)

MACBUSH: Wait! Stop! Where are they? Damn! There's more I need
To know! Gone. "Burning food": it makes no sense!
Halt! Who goes there?

(*Enter AIDE.*)

AIDE: It's only me, Sir, I—I followed you.

MACBUSH: Saw you the three weird preachers?

AIDE: No, my lord.

MACBUSH: Why did you follow me?

AIDE: My lord, I came
To tell you the great lords MacDole and Kempf
Accept your invitation. They're enroute
To Kenn O'Bunk right now.

MACBUSH (*slowly coming to his senses*): To Kenn O'Bunk?

AIDE: Aye, my good lord.

MACBUSH: Aha, that's good.
We'll go there, too. Soon TIME, and NEWSWEEK, too
Will tell my dread exploits. Let no one doubt
My manhood now—but from this moment on
My hand will speak the wishes of my heart.
I'll crown my thoughts with acts—let nature rule—
And do the deed before the purpose cool!
Now no more talk! (*To AIDE*): Where are these gentlemen?
Come, bring me where they are.

(*Exit MACBUSH and AIDE. Flames flicker on. Street sounds rise & fade.*)

ACT IV

SCENE THREE

(*The same. Enter the TWO HOMELESS PEOPLE, attracted by the fire. They warm themselves gratefully at the can.*)

HOMELESS WOMAN: Someone forgot to turn off the front burner.

HOMELESS MAN: It's our good luck. I've always said, with all
The documents they shred and burn each day
In ministries and government bureaus,
Their print shops, copy rooms, and registries:
If they would take the faded dollar bills,
Memos, transcripts, expense account receipts,
The phone call logs, etcetera, and not
Incinerate them in tall stacks—

WOMAN: The ones
That coat the penthouse pools with ashes!

MAN: That's right; if they'd decentralize the burning,
And put the fire down here where it can warm
The likes of you and me. Those documents
They mark TOP SECRET—

WOMAN: Like the Declaration
of Independence, or the Bill of Rights—

MAN: I'd like to get one in my hands, but not
To pry, you know. I only want to measure
Their fuel value . . .

(*They pick up some of the scattered papers and feed the fire.*)

WOMAN: You'd think these folks'd have the smarts not to
Record this stuff—look, here's an airplane log:
From Colombia via Costa Rica to
Miami—this could be the smoking gun,
The missing document! We could be rich!

(*She throws it in the fire.*)

MAN: And how 'bout this? The Spy Chief—he just died—
I wonder what his autograph is worth?

(*He throws it in the fire.*)

WOMAN (*conspiratorially*): I hear some squirming in the audience:

Some whispers, paper rustling, reaching for
Their handkerchiefs . . . They check their playbills, wond'ring
Why these homeless people keep returning to
The stage.

MAN (*Oratorically*): What place do vagrants have
In plush theatres or gilded leather books
By the great Bard, full of the rise and fall
Of kings and queens, aristocrats,
The ebb and wane of wars—what place is there
For homeless people on the stage of history?

(*He approaches audience, threateningly, like a beggar in a bus terminal.*)

Come, take a look—a touch—don't turn away:
I could be you, or I could be the soldier,
Gone mad now, who fought your last misguided war,
And she could be the surrogate mom
Who bore your babe while you climbed up the ladder.

(*He brandishes a torn paper he has picked up*):

Here, check our pedigrees:
Find yesterday's aristocrat without
A nickel in a land where wealth and power
Come overnight to tenement landlords,
To pushers, inside traders, baseball players—

(*He has mounted an old crate and declaims, Hyde Park style, to an audience of one, who supplies the clapping.*)

—and we,
Unnoticed as we are, yet we see all:
The imminence of great Macbush's fall—The hint, the puff, of scandal, that doth presage
The bigger storm—like the faint breeze that rustles
The silk curtain two hours before
The cyclone fells the house.
Led by MacDole and Kempf, the opposition
Is in New Hampshire, burning for revenge.
Full one-third of the Senate, and all the House,

Are watching whether Macbush's coat-tails
Will pull them along, or trip his own legs up.

(*The two return to conversing by the fire.*)

WOMAN: And what's the tyrant up to?

MAN: As for him,
He's making strident speeches, issuing
Decrees . . . in secret, authorizing more
Covert activity, and making deals
To gut environmental regulations.
Meanwhile he's scrambling to please everyone—
Death camp survivors, Polish labor leaders,
Invoking everybody's favorite ghost,
From William Loeb to Martin Luther King,
From Jesus Christ to David Ben Gurion.
Then he repairs to Kenn O'Bunk where he
Can be photographed jogging on the beach
Like a dead Kennedy . . .

WOMAN: Some say he's mad.
Others, who like him more, say he just works
To push th' agenda of old King Ronald farther.
Some say he's proving something, but, 'tis sure
He can't zip up his manhood in the state
It's in.

MAN: Now does he feel his secret mischiefs
Stick to his hands. Now every day a new
Revolt begins in his own troops. And those
He orders only follow orders, not
Their hearts. Macbush now feels his cloak hang loose
Like a giant's robe upon a dwarfish thief.
Meanwhile, the Democrats are marching on,
Calling themselves the medicine we need
To purge the country of its sickness.

WOMAN: Ha!
They're all the same to us. Now who can blame
Us for our scattered senses, that recoil

From taking part in their condemnéd world?
We may be crazy, but we're not stupid.

MAN (*looking around*): 'Tis morning.

WOMAN: The cars arrive.

MAN: To th' sidewalk, then.
To greet the workers in their morn rush hour,
Like weeds that push up 'mid the sovereign flowers.

(*Exit the two* HOMELESS PEOPLE. *Flames die; bright daylight comes, and fades.*)

ACT V
☆☆☆☆☆

SCENE ONE

Kenn O'Bunk. The next night. Muted trumpets, sea sounds, gulls. The sounds fade as MACBUSH enters his library. He flops into an easy chair. MACBUSH'S AIDE enters after.

AIDE: What's Your Grace's pleasure, Sire?

MACBUSH: Tell me
The news, the polls: what do they say?

AIDE: It's as
We feared; you're slipping. Our projections show
You losing big. Though you're incumbent, sir,
You just don't have the ratings yet—you're like
A TV pilot show whose demographics
Are unclear: the sponsors do not buy; they fear
Whoe'er the other networks run against you
Is sure to win more viewers.

MACBUSH: I won't give up!
Though we're surrounded, I can hole up here.
They'll have to smoke me out! Bring me my six-gun!

AIDE: 'Tis not needed yet.

MACBUSH: I'll put it on now. Go, and let me know
When all the guests arrive.

AIDE: I will, my lord. (*Exit AIDE*)

MACBUSH: To hell with news; it matters not to me!
Till burning food to Kenn O'Bunk doth come,
What need I fear? Lord Kempf? The great MacDole?
Are they not whole men? Not entire? Or are
They New Age souls, Aquarians, in whom
The female hormones grow, and make 'em gentle?

(*MACBUSH flicks on TV. The THREE TELEVANGELISTS are*

there. Volume is low. MACBUSH exhibits some dissatisfaction with the program.)

(*Knocking on door.*)

MACBUSH: Come in. (*Enter PSYCHIATRIST*)

Ah, Doctor. Come in; have a seat. How is our patient, Doctor?

DOCTOR: Not so sick.
My lord, "sick's" not the word. She just needs sleep.
She's troubled, as I told you, by these visions
That make her sleepwalk, keep her from her rest,
And fill her heart with fear.

MACBUSH: The TV show?

DOCTOR: Yes, sir.

MACBUSH: It's all my fault.
I never should have told her of this program.
It's got me, too, but in a different way . . .
The message is contagious, like a fever.
They get you when you're down, lonely, lukewarm,
And most impressionable, and then later
You find you can't go on without 'em. . . .
Can we not find these ministers diseased,
And pluck them from the TV screen, rub out
Their image and their sources of support,
And with some sweet, oblivious antidote—
Like Mister Rogers' Neighborhood reruns—
Clean up the video of that perilous stuff
That weighs upon the heart?

DOCTOR: Looks like the ministers are doing that
To themselves. Their revenues are down;
Their share of captured homes is falling off.

(*Door bell rings; chime to the tune of "Hail to the Chief."*)

MACBUSH: Well,
I've got to go, Doc; keep your eyes on her.
And while you're at it, put this country on
Your couch, and figure out what's bugging it.

Check out our symptoms; tell us our disease.
Did your guru, Dr. Freud, write anything
On nations growing up? Were we abused
By Washington and Jefferson, our dads,
When we were young, or have we seen too much
Domestic violence? Are we bulemic
As a country, alternately gorging and
Puking out the world's resources—
Or is it something in the water, Doc?
Do you think we all should go on lithium
To save the world from our behavioral extremes?

DOCTOR: Good Lord, I wish I knew. . . .

MACBUSH: Well, go find out, and let me know.
(*Exit DOCTOR.*) Meanwhile,
I reign till to these ailments we succumb.
Or:
Till burning food to Kenn O'Bunk doth come.
Whichever happens first.

(*Door bell chimes again. AIDE rushes back in with* MACBUSH'S *gun and holster.*)

AIDE: Your six-guns, sir.

MACBUSH: What for?

AIDE: You asked for them.

MACBUSH: Oh, later, later. Go answer the door. (*Chime.*)

AIDE: Yes, Sire. (*Exit AIDE.*)

(*Chimes. MACBUSH in deepening shadow, his lips faintly moving, whispering*):

MACBUSH: Wake Ronald with your ringing; I wish you could.

(*Fade to black.*)

ACT V

SCENE TWO

(The same night. The TV studio of Act I, Scene One. Enter the THREE TELEVANGELISTS.)

THIRD TELEVANGELIST (*hanging up his coat*):
We are departing from the script again!
We have come back to play one final scene,
Though there's no precedent for our return
In any ancient text. When last we met
With King Macbush, we were supposed to vanish
In a puff of smoke—
But having so ingratiated ourselves
With you thus far, we knew you wouldn't like
To see us leave without a last good-bye.

SECOND: In short, we talked it over backstage and
Decided to come back, and be up front with you.

FIRST (*sitting on the corner of a table or desk*):
Look, you're obviously well-heeled, no?
You've coughed up twenty bucks for a theatre ticket;
You prob'ly ate some Thai food first, and put
It on your MasterCard. But: you've been through
Hard times; you know they sometimes hit us all.
We need your help; you know our situation,
I don't have to tell ya just how bad it is—

SECOND: Right on. Tell them, brother—

FIRST: I am. (*Louder*): You folks have read the news!
You know
The devil runs the newspapers—he loves
To print those full-page headlines trumpeting
Our weaknesses! It makes his own work easier.

THIRD: Now, we're not askin' for ourselves—we need

Funds for our educational programs,
For our spiritual, humanitarian aid
We send to guys with names like Juan and Pedro
Fighting for *you,* down in the trenches of
Latino Land.

FIRST: If you can find it in
Your hearts—

(*Telephone rings.*)

Excuse me—

(*He answers the phone.*)

Oh, Shit! It's Him again!

(*He punches the executive conference-call button. Enter, as* VOICE, *THE MAN UPSTAIRS.*)

VOICE: There you go again! (*The three cower.*)
I told you, long ago—Act Three, Scene Four—
I never, never, N,E,V,E,R,
Authorized you in My name, or in the name
Of any of My scriptural revelations,
To involve yourselves and all your churches in
This Contra War—it should have been enough
I let you spread your sugarplum gospel
To the barefoot poor of the Americas—
Now feel my wrath—

(*Special effects: drums, lights flickering—*)

You three, whom Destiny—
That runs this world and all who walk on it—
Hath caused to be belched up from your dressing room,
Back to the stage you briefly did inhabit,
You being most unfit to change your clothes
And exit to the alley, all scot-free!
Your God is angry! Hear Me! Tell your flocks
Whom you by your words have enflamed against
All spiritual diversity: Know this:
However men and women approach Me,

I do accept them, for the path they take
From every side is Mine! And in the end
I will receive all good and righteous people,
Not caring whom they worshipped, prayed to, praisèd,
Or sacrificed to in their fleeting lives!
Now know the punishment I deal to you,
To chastize your misguided zealotry!

(*The door to the television studio is kicked in. A small peasant army—three or four Central American farmers—enters, accompanied by a female Nicaraguan soldier in full blue battle dress, carrying an automatic weapon. They subdue the* THREE TELEVANGELISTS, *who try to reach pistols in their desk drawers, and try to reach the phone. Next to enter is a Catholic* PRIEST*—a liberation theologian—wearing black pants, a black short-sleeved shirt, and a clerical collar. He is carrying a weapon and smoking a cigarette. He speaks with a Spanish accent.*)

SECOND TELEVANGELIST (*struggling*): I told you this would happen!
We should have stuck to domestic issues,
Like abortion, TV violence, and sex!

THIRD TELEVANGELIST: Be quiet!

PRIEST: Relax, you three. Leave off your struggle. I
And these my friends are ministers as well.
Your guns are useless—bulletless; you may
As easily fire at the wind, or wound
The ocean wave, as try to harm one straw
That's in their hats. We are not here to hurt you.
If you could dial 911,
If anyone would help you now, your phones
Are all unplugged. Your TV station's dark.
Now listen—this is why we're here—you three
And scores of others in your shadowy group,
From ex-generals to wheeler-dealers in
The palace basement did conspire
To violate the constitutional restraint—
The separation of the church and state.
You, and the military, and the most

Clandestine powers of th'executive branch,
Did seek to overturn the humble gains
Of these poor folk, denying their most basic
human rights: a safe home, food to eat, and land
To farm in peace. We've come from far away.
Now let me introduce our little group,
Our bible-study base community.
We all have wanted to meet you for some time.

FIRST PEASANT (*holding a photograph. As he speaks the photo is also projected above them as a slide.*):
Hello. My name is Mario Godoy. This is a picture of my daughter, Isabel. I want you to come to visit our village. I will show you the place where she was murdered on her wedding day, with her fianceé, and mother—how do you call it—in-law? Then they burned her. It was the soldiers you raise money for. You come and I will show you. One of the contra dropped this pamphlet from your church.

SECOND PEASANT (*holding a photo, the slide projected*):
My name is Carlos. I am pleased to meet you. This is a picture of my son Pedrito. This is his baseball glove. He was coming home from the practice. He had his baseball shirt full of mangos he has picked for his mamá. He stepped on a mine. All he ever wanted to do was to become a third baseman and travel to Cincinatti to play for the great Pete Rose. Come: I will show you the place.

THIRD PEASANT: (*Holding a photo—the slide projected—of Ben Linder*):
My name is María de los Dolores. Yo soy una campesina de Cuá. I am a woman from Cuá. This is a picture of my friend, Ben. He was a gringo. You have met him? Here is a newspaper photo of him on his unicycle in the circus. He was bringing electricity to our town when he was killed. My other friend saw it happen. You come and you can talk to her. Maybe you can help us finish the project, no? You come.

PRIEST: We'd better go now. (*Beckoning the TELEVANGELISTS to rise.*)
You are coming, too.

We will not hurt you. All we want to do
Is show you all the ruin you have caused
In our country, in your God's name. You will be
A special kind of tourist, treated with
Politeness and respect proportional to
The influence you hold here. But you will
Come. Now. All of you. And then we'll bring
You back to tell your people about your trip.

THIRD TELEVANGELIST: Er, this is very nice of you,
But I can't go. I am a candidate
For the highest office in the land. I would
Be missed at the debates and caucuses.

PRIEST: To be a viable candidate, you know,
You must go on a foreign junket. We'll
Have many photo opportunities.

FIRST TELEVANGELIST: You've got the wrong guy, Pal; if you'll excuse me,
I gave up politics last week—

(*The THREE TELEVANGELISTS are borne bodily out the door. All exit except the PRIEST.*)

PRIEST: You in your seats: the theatre is not locked.
Some one who wants to, run, you're free, go tell
The cop on the street that these three ministers
Were kidnapped in a terrorist attack.
Go—phone one of the great lords of your land,
Some master of the air force or the navy,
Perhaps this is the pretext they have sought
To mount invasion of our tiny country.
Go—set up roadblocks, seal the borders, you
Won't find us; we are traveling in reverse
The hidden railroad that has brought so many
Salvadorans to sanctuary here.
Go, someone; sound th'alarm. But, wait: hold on:
If there's no hurry, stay here in your seat.
If the short-term disappearance of these three
Is no great loss, sit back. If you believe

They're in no danger—and they're not—relax
And watch the last scenes; see what fate awaits
Macbush, the man who wanted to be King.

(*Exit PRIEST, straightening up the office as he goes, closing door softly. Black-out.*)

ACT V

SCENE THREE

(*Outside the palace at Kenn O'Bunk. Later the same night. Enter MACDOLE and KEMPF, out for some fresh air.*)

MACDOLE: The air bites shrewdly; it is very cold.

KEMPF (*jogging and sparring to keep warm*):
It is a nipping and an eager air.

MACDOLE: What's the hour?

KEMPF: It's just struck eight.

MACDOLE (*scanning the horizon*): Indeed? I heard it not. 'Tis almost time.

KEMPF: Is all made ready?

MACDOLE: Aye.

KEMPF: Shhh. Someone comes.

(*Enter a local FISHERMAN, in boots, foul weather gear, a pipe, and full white beard. He speaks with heavy down-east accent.*)

FISHERMAN: Ahoy!

MACDOLE & KEMPF: How now?

(*Sounds of revelry echo from within the palace.*)

FISHERMAN: I thought there might be some disturbance, sirs.
Those sounds, my Lords; what are they?

KEMPF: The King doth hold a pep rally tonight,
With drinking toasts, and clapping on the back.
And as he drains his drafts of lite beer down,
The cap-gun and the bugle do proclaim
His readiness for battle.

FISHERMAN: He's dressed for war?

MACDOLE: Why, no, man; he is in his topsiders,
His khakis, Izod shirt, and yachting cap.

FISHERMAN: Well.
To my mind, though I'm native here, and not
To th' manor born, it is a costume that's
More honored on the beach, or on the dock . . .
I tell you, sirs, this partying east and west
Makes us traduced and taxed by other nations . . .
'Tis one great frolic
From the volleyball and surf of San Diego
To th' cocktail parties at marinas here.
You can't but wonder who's minding the store,
Who's baiting all the traps. . . . It's plain to see
Th'economy is heading for a fall.
To borrow and to borrow and to borrow,
At this excessive pace from day to day . . .
What with the loss of manufacturing,
And third world debt default, we've got no money
Coming in. We're in debt now. And on the day
The bills come due, someone'll have to pay.

(*Noise of revelry increases. Lights, as from a door thrown open. MACBUSH'S voice, without.*)

MACBUSH: MacDole! Lord Kempf! You're missing all the toasts!

MACBUSH: We come, your Highness! (*To the FISHERMAN*):
Friend, we thank you for
Your thoughts, which weigh on our minds, too. Adieu.

(*Exit MACDOLE & KEMPF. FISHERMAN stands, smoking pipe. Fade-out.*)

ACT V

SCENE FOUR

The same night. Within the palace at Kenn O'Bunk. Various revelers and party-goers. The scene has the packaged hilarity of a Miller Lite commercial. Enter MACBUSH, expansively, with arms around MACDOLE and KEMPF.

MACBUSH:. . . And here's the two I find most dear to me!
No president, no king, in history
Had ever two more able ministers
To fill his ears with good advice—the one
A crack economist, the other a
Straight-shooting, honest-talking mouthpiece of
Our country's heartland. Come now, fill your cups.
Then we'll sit down. Give me some lite beer, please.

(*All drink. MACDOLE and KEMPF taste the beer.*)

MACBUSH: Ahh! What do you think?

(*The two, as if delivering weighty advice*):

MACDOLE: Tastes great.

KEMPF: Less filling.

MACBUSH: There! What'd I tell ya? These two gentlemen
Are the bedrock of our country and our party.
They draw the hand of John and Jane Doe to our lever
In the voting booth. Who doubts for a minute
We'll win another landslide in November?

(*Strained silence. A few desultory claps.*)

A toast to all! And to our queen who's resting,
Unable to attend. And to our new
Vice-President, who's back in Washington,
Burning the midnight oil.
Now where's the entertainment? I thought we
Had hired Rosenshontz and Gould & Stearns
To fill the room with song and funny stories!

AIDE: I'm sorry, Sir. They're booked to perform at
The opposition gala.

MACBUSH: What of it?
We'll entertain ourselves. Hey, look who's here—
I want you all to meet my good friend "Juan
García"—we go back a long way, don't we?

(MACBUSH *grandly plucks from the crowd a burly Latin-American with bushy hair, gold chains on his hairy chest, shirt open at the collar, wearing several large gold rings.*)

GARCIA: We sure do, Chief.

MACBUSH: What brings you here? Of course—
Can't talk about it, huh? Hush-hush? (He winks.)

GARCIA: That's right.

MACBUSH: Well. Let's eat.

(MACBUSH *claps his hands. Each actor vanishes momentarily into the shadows, returning with a dinner-table chair. They line the chairs up in one tight row facing the audiences. No table. With the actors' return,* KING RONALD *returns as well, still clad in his sleeper and carrying his stuffed animal. He also carries a chair, which he places in the middle of the row, and sits down. The other guests can not see him. He is invisible to all but* MACBUSH.)

AIDE: Sit down, my lord.

MACBUSH: Is this some kind of joke?

AIDE: May't please your highness, sit.

MACBUSH: The table's full.

AIDE (*indicating KING RONALD'S chair*):
Here is a place reserved, sir.

MACBUSH: Where?

AIDE: Here, my good lord. What is't that moves you, Sire?

(*KING RONALD appears to yawn, to stretch, to cuddle with the teddy, to sleep. He lies prone upon the laps of four or five people along the row of chairs. They do not notice him.*)

MACBUSH: Thou canst not say I did it! Never suck
Thy thumb at me!

AIDE: Gentlemen, rise. His highness is not well.

(*They all rise instantly, dumping KING RONALD to the floor. They do not notice. KING RONALD stands and exits, as if sleep-walking. MACBUSH stares after him.*)

AIDE: Sit, worthy friends; my lord is often thus,
And hath been for some years—'tis a flashback
Of LSD he accidentally took
When the Agency ran drug experiments—
I pray you, sit, the fit is momentary,
Try not to notice, or you'll make it worse.

(*They all sit down. MACBUSH sits, too, in the now-empty chair.*)

(*AIDE stands behind MACBUSH'S chair, whispering in his ear.*)

AIDE: Are you a man?

MACBUSH: Of course I am; what of it?

AIDE: Then stop behaving like a campfire girl
Who's frightened by a counselor's ghostly story!

MACBUSH: You'd shiver, too, if you had seen what I
Just saw.

AIDE: Sire, don't get all bent out of shape:
You were but looking at an empty chair!

(*MACBUSH is worked up, fidgeting—*)

MACBUSH: Where is my wife?

AIDE: I don't know, sir.

MACBUSH: My friends,
Relax; I have a strange infirmity—
'Tis nothing much to those who know me well.
Come, here's good health to all!

ALL: Here's to you, King.

(*Re-enter KING RONALD. Only MACBUSH sees him. He rises in self-defense.*)

MACBUSH: Avaunt! and quit my sight! Go back to bed!

AIDE: All rise, I pray you—

(*They all stand up. MACBUSH crouches on his chair, hugging the back.*)

AIDE: Please sit, friends; this will pass.

(*They all sit.*)

(*KING RONALD approaches MACBUSH'S chair. He tugs at MACBUSH'S sleeve, pulling him gently but with great force from his chair. The chair falls over. All the guests rise simultaneously. MACBUSH is on the floor struggling with an opponent only he can see.*)

AIDE: Sit, please. (*Guests all sit.*)

MACBUSH: Help! No more! Thou canst not walk—thine eyes
Are closed—I tucked you in myself!
The devil get you gone; take any shape
But that: I'll fight you like a man! Be gone!

(*Exit KING RONALD.*)

MACDOLE: My lord, what's eating you?

MACBUSH: How can you all
Just sit there, like you're on a subway car,
Talking, chewing, keeping your natural color,
Just minding your own business while your king
Is fighting for his life!

KEMPF: With what, my lord?
With whom?

AIDE: I pray you, friends, question him not—
The fit grows worse and worse. Get up and go.
Don't daily at the door, but go at once.

(*They all rise. Exit* AIDE *with a few guests.* MACDOLE *and* KEMPF *exit more slowly, eyeing* MACBUSH.)

GUEST: Good night, and better health attend His Majesty!

(MACBUSH *is on floor, choking back sobs.* GARCÍA *stands over him.*)

MACBUSH: What time is it?

GARCIA: It's just past midnight, King.

(GARCÍA *speaks with a heavy Latin-American accent.*)

MACBUSH: It will have blood, they say. Blood will have blood.
Stones, parrots, tape recorders will spill our secrets.
It is an evil time, García, when
The mansion cracks, the walls collapse, and all
We've hidden sees the light of day—

GARCIA: Macbush,
These are a leetle girl's words, not the brave
Pronouncements of a man.

MACBUSH: Easy for you
To say: there's no mistaking where
Your hormones point. You're macho to the core—
From a swamp-infested land where men are men:
They curse, they spit, they swing their machetes
With equal ease at jungle vines, or snakes,
Or human limbs. Is there no way, García,
For me to get to be a man like you?

GARCIA: In the country where I come from, amigo,
There ees a simple test a man can take.
It wards off evil spirits, too, like the ones
You just have wrestled with.

MACBUSH: What is it, man?

GARCIA: Open your mouth!

MACBUSH: It's something I must eat?

(GARCÍA *shakes some salt into his hand. He flings it into* MACBUSH'S *mouth.*)

MACBUSH: That's all?

GARCIA: No, hombre. Keep it open.

(*He pours a shot of aguardiente—white rum—and mutters a pidgin pre-columbian prayer. He pours the drink into* MACBUSH'S *mouth.*)

MACBUSH: Ohh!
(*He coughs and swallows the dose. Now he is elated.*)
I did it! No big thing! I mean, no problem!

GARCIA: Silencio! Now this:
(*He dangles a large red pepper in front of* MACBUSH. MACBUSH *hesitates.*)
Take a beeg bite,
King, like a man—

(MACBUSH *bites off and chews a large piece of the pepper. He quickly stares, immobilized by a double horror—the fiery taste and the fulfillment of the prophecy. He tries to speak. His words come hot and difficult.*)

MACBUSH: Oh, hot!
A curse upon those fiends who spoke
The truth in riddles!
Fear not, they said, till burning food
To Kenn O'Bunk doth come, and now 'tis come.
If this means what I think, what I most fear,
There's no escaping, and no staying here.
My aide! My six-gun, quick! Blow, wind; quake, land,
At least we'll die with pistol in our hand!

(*He starts off, comes back to give* GARCÍA *a quick abrazo—an embrace. Exit* MACBUSH.)

GARCIA: Why all the fuss, man? You're one mean gringo.
He passed the test; he ate the jalapeño.
(*He licks some salt, eats the rest of the pepper, and drinks a shot, toasting the audience.*)
The king, he would not hug me if he knew
The leetle job they called me here to do.

(*Exit* GARCÍA.)

ACT V

SCENE FIVE

(*The same night. Outside the palace at Kenn O'Bunk. Wind and surf noise, increasing, as in a storm. Enter* MACBUSH, *fanning his mouth. He wears his capgun-and-holster.*)

MACBUSH: This taste that's in my mouth: it isn't fear.
My senses are not chilled; my hair stands not
On end! I'm ready; nothing scares me now.

(*Enter* AIDE.)

AIDE: The queen, my lord, is gone.

MACBUSH: Gone?

AIDE: Gone. She left
This forwarding address: "Golden Valley
Apotheosis Second Coming
Four-Square Family Tent Camp, Alabama."

MACBUSH: She could have gone there later.
Tomorrow, or the next day, or the next.
She couldn't hack this creepy place another day.
Now I feel like a shadow, an ex-player
That struts his stuff during the half-time show

And then is heard no more. It's like a tale
Told by a sportscaster, chock full of sound
And fury, signifying—nothing!
Go! Leave—I'll call you when I need you.

AIDE: Yes, Sir. (*Exit AIDE.*)

MACBUSH: At least the other prophecy still holds:
No whole man is a threat to me—
(*Enter MACDOLE and KEMPF.*)
How now, what do you want? I fear you not!
Come on, make my day!

KEMPF: *Your* days are done! Your throne rejects you now!

MACBUSH: Have at you, Kempf! Put up your dukes,
MacDole—
Damn him that cries, "Have mercy on my soul!"

(*They wrestle.*)

MACBUSH: Away, you fools! You waste your strength! You may
As well take potshots at the sea,
Or wrestle with the churning sand! Go choose
A target you can hurt. I bear a charmed life—
Only a man who's not entire can harm me!

MACDOLE: Then kiss your charm good-bye, my king, for I
Am not a whole man. Fascist fire blew out
My best arm in the Great War!

KEMPF: And look at me—
You see a warrior you think complete,
But I am best known as a quarter-back!

MACBUSH: Accursèd be the tongues that tell me so!
For you have cow'd the manhood I just won.
And curses on those weird preachers again,
Who spoke in tongues, and prophesied in riddles.
I'll not fight with thee.

MACDOLE: Then yield thee, coward,
And know what's still in store. No patriot
Would want to see our country wracked again

By having yet another president leave
His throne in shame and scandal. While we suspect
The means you used t'ascend yourself,
And though you've brought us to the brink of ruin,
We do not mean to see you live to be
The butt of TV talk show jokes, and cartoons
On the Op-Ed page, for by association
It would harm our Party, too.

KEMPF: Therefore we've planned
A painless martyrdom for you. We've sent
Our emissaries to make a secret deal.
The world will know you as the king who sent
Himself across the sea as ransom for
His countrymen who languished, hostages
To a vengeful, fundamentalist regime.
In future times, your name will spill from lips
Tightened in war. Remember the Alamo!

MACDOLE: Remember the Maine!

KEMPF: Remember Pearl Harbor!

MACDOLE: Forget Vietnam!

BOTH: Remember Macbush!

KEMPF: —will be the battle cry
When brave Judeo-Christian soldiers go
To grapple with the desert Moslem hordes,
As Merlin prophesied so long ago.

(*Wind and surf sound increase. The sound of a jet engine revs in the near distance. Enter* GARCÍA *and* MACBUSH'S AIDE.)

MACBUSH: You? Et tu, my Aide? Then fall, Macbush!

(*He swoons.* GARCÍA *and* AIDE *carry* MACBUSH *off.*)

MACDOLE (*to the audience*):
Don't worry, friends; Macbush is safe. We've picked
The finest flight crew you can find, with years
Of flying missions all unknown to you.
This same crew served in Cuban skies above

The Bay of Pigs. Some say, though it will be
Denied, they flew with Che Guevara's corpse
Over the mountains of Bolivia—
And rumors tell they brought the chopper in
To ferry young prince Bobby K
From Marilyn's deathbed. For years they've flown
The milk-run flights in old prop planes somewhere
Where Nicaragua meets Honduras,
With weapons in and cocaine out. Now, they
Take off on their most secret trip, leaving
Macbush to keep the mullahs company,
And coming back with hostages released
From lonely dungeons in the east—

(*Surf and wind up. Engine rev turns to roar. Spotlight travels across audience, to lip of stage, up actors' bodies, up and away—indicating jet's take-off. Wind. Engine fades. Storm rises.* KEMPF *and* MACDOLE *watch the disappearing plane, as rain lashes their trenchcoats.*)

KEMPF: Macbush, our king, is gone.

MACDOLE: Round up the usual suspects.

BOTH: Aye, aye! (*They shake hands, salute each other, and exit to either side of the stage. Storm, surf, gulls, buoy bells, foghorn, fade to black.*)

ACT V

SCENE SIX

(*On national television, beamed from the palace throne room. 'Hail to the Chief'' played at slow tempo. Enter the new President,* QUEEN ELIZABETH MACDOLE. *She may be played by the* MACDOLE *actor wearing a wig. Dressed in the same suit, he has exchanged his trousers for a skirt.*)

QUEEN ELIZABETH: My fellow Americans, let me be
The anchorwoman of your news tonight.
We shall not spend a large expense of time,
Because we've much to do. As someone said,
When sorrows come, they come not single-spies
But in battalions. Today, so many great
Events took place, the wire service jammed
And seized up, like a river choked with logs.
First the good news: our hostages are freed!
The how and why's a secret, not yet known
Even to me. All these we welcome back
To our great national nuclear family.
There's sad and ominous news as well:
Three ministers of God, three bright beacons
Of hope and faith to lonely TV viewers,
Have vanished from their studio without
A trace. No stone will be unturned: We've put
Our best investigators on the case;
Their terrorist kidnappers will be caught.
As for the rumors you've all heard by now,
Of a Navy task force steaming toward
The Persian Gulf, and U.S. soldiers fighting
Upon Iranian ground—I have no comment:
Denial *or* confirmation would endanger
Our vital national security.
I've saved the most momentous news for last.
Your king, your president, the great Macbush,
Is dead, or rather, M.I.A. I speak
To you tonight not as vice-president,
But as your monarch. (*Music up: "The Star-Spangled Banner," muffled.*)
I mean to be the queen
Of all the people—now let my first decree
Be a sad and *doleful* one: let grief begin
For great Macbush, that Honorable man,
For he was likely, had he but stayed on,
To have proved most royally; and, for his passage,
The soldiers' music and the rites of war
Speak loudly for him!

Go, bid the soldiers shoot.
(*A 21-gun salute begins, continuing through the speech.*)
My fellow citizens, the system works.
The crown sits on a woman's head;
The sceptre's wielded by a distaff hand—
There is survivability of command!

(*Cheers. Trumpets: "Hail to the Chief." Exit QUEEN. Cut back to the conclusion of Our National Anthem, while the slow 21-gun salute continues.*)

(*Enter TWO HOMELESS PERSONS, responding to the speech they have heard broadcast over street public-address system.*)

HOMELESS WOMAN: What crap!

HOMELESS MAN: You think so, too?

HOMELESS WOMAN: I mean, what happens
To women who ascend the throne? Why do
They all turn into Uncle Toms?

HOMELESS MAN: You mean
"Aunt Maggies?" I don't know.

WOMAN: Maybe it's a germ.
"The Center for Disease Control Today
Identified a new and fatal virus,
Afflicting female politicians who've
Been intimate with men who previously
Engaged in public service . . ."

MAN: I suppose
You'd do it different if you took the throne?

WOMAN: I would; I know I would.

MAN: Well, take it.

WOMAN: What?

(*The HOMELESS MAN brings out a crate; sets it in the middle of the stage.*)

MAN: The throne is yours. Now make your speech.

WOMAN: But I—

MAN (*Officiously, wheeling a pretend camera into position, focusing*):
Your majesty,
You're on the air. An anxious country awaits
Your speech. A nation of skinned knees is wailing
For the ointment of your words.

(*She ascends the throne. She adjusts her threadbare clothes. She speaks, first hesitating, then settling in, then powerfully*):

WOMAN: My fellow countrypersons, stop and listen.
Don't be afraid; I speak to you tonight
Not as a homeless woman—I'm
Your monarch: the first you've had who wore the crown
And wore a dress at the same time (except
in private!). Awesome news has shook us up
Today. I don't intend to gloss it over,
To patch it with a superficial dressing
That lets the gross infection fester on
Beneath the surface. Instead, as queen, I mean
To treat all of our pains at their deep source—
Something none of our leaders has tried before.
A woman's place is in the house: The White House.
And while I live here, let there be no one
Homeless in our country: our top priority
Will be shelter—a home and healthy food—
For all who live out in the streets, and for
The other homeless ones: the exiles
And refugees who've fled death squads and armies
Run amock. Which brings me to our next decree:
Dear friends, our capital is strewn
With shrines of stones, to citizens whose lives
Ended abruptly—war prevented them
From playing out their dreams, life's natural course.
I speak of the Unknown Soldier, and of
The Vietnam Vets' black memorial. . . .
Tonight we are at war again, although
You may not know it—no peal of bells,

No marching band, no act of Congress called
Us all to arms. We will not shoulder guns;
Instead, we're asked by social sacrifice
To render up the funds to fortify
Our palace walls thrice-over, and to ignore
The distant victims, and the ones at home,
Of our perpetual state of siege. Tonight,
We move to change all that:
We here renounce all clandestine support
For institutional terrorist regimes—
Let every death squad, every torturer know,
Henceforth no person can vanish from their home
Without a personal pang afflicting
This woman's breast in our national palace!
And as a monument to this resolve,
I propose we build a new memorial
On our esplanade: to all the Disappeared
Of the seventies and eighties:
Build it of cardboard, wire, tin, to make
Us think of shanties the world over,
Too flimsy to keep out the weather,
Too weak to resist a soldier's boot at midnight.
Then cover it with photos like the ones
The Mothers brandish in the streets, of sons
And daughters disappeared, of peasants, teachers,
Singers, union leaders, and place among them
The face of our own missing king, Macbush,
For he
Was "E Pluribus Unum"—only one
of many!

(*During her speech, the other actors have returned to the stage, all now unrecognizably dressed as homeless people appearing from the shadows. They form an audience for her. They sway to the cadence of her speech. She continues*):

Now, my fellow countrypersons,
We have not spent a large expense of time;
I have not come to beg, but to embrace you.
Good night to all at once and to each one,

Whom we invite to visit Washington.
In the coming days we've much to do, to say,
Long live world peace, and UP THE E.R.A!

(*Lights slowly fade as someone crowns her with some aluminum scrap—a pie plate; someone else puts a rolled-up newspaper in her upraised hand and lights it for a torch. The choir of* HOMELESS PEOPLE, *gathered for a moment and about to disperse to the shadows, sings*):

From the mountains
To the prairies,
To the oceans
White with foam,
God bless America,
My Home Sweet Home.

(*Black-out.*)

If you liked MACBUSH, you may also want to read the award-winning play, A PEASANT OF EL SALVADOR, by Peter Gould and Stephen Stearns. A PEASANT OF EL SALVADOR has been acclaimed as the most powerful and effective educational drama ever written in the United States on a Latin American theme. For your personal copy, send $7.00 to:

PEASANT
Whetstone Books
P.O. Box 355
Brattleboro, Vermont 05301

(Also available at your local bookstore—distributed by INLAND BOOKS.)

☆ ☆

Peter Gould is half of Gould & Stearns, Vermont's well-known theatre duo, who have delighted audiences all over the United States since 1980. Gould & Stearns represented the U.S. at the 1980 Mexican-International Mime Festival, and toured Honduras in 1987 as cultural ambassadors for Parners Of The Americas.
The Gould & Stearns repertoire includes: a family mime-theatre hour; a full-length adult evening show of physical comedy, vaudeville, story, and song; and—now in its seventh year—the unforgettable docu-drama, A PEASANT OF EL SALVADOR. For information, contact:

Gould & Stearns
RD 2 Box 62
West Brattleboro, Vermont 05301
802-254-8355